HOLY FIRE

Also by Daniel Halpern

Poetry

Traveling on Credit
The Lady Knife-Thrower
Street Fire
Life Among Others
Seasonal Rights
Tango
Foreign Neon
Selected Poems

Translations

The Song of Mririda, by Mririda n'Aït Attik
Orchard Lamps, by Ivan Drach (co-translator)

Editor

Borges on Writing (co-editor)
The American Poetry Anthology
The Antaeus Anthology
The Art of the Tale: An International Anthology of Short Stories
On Nature
Writers on Artists
Reading the Fights (co-editor)
Our Private Lives: Journals, Notebooks and Diaries
Plays in One Act
The Sophisticated Cat (co-editor)
Dante's Inferno: Translations by 20 Contemporary Poets
The Autobiographical Eye
On Music (co-editor)

Food

The Good Food: Soup, Stews and Pastas (with Julie Strand)
Halpern's Guide to the Essential Restaurants of Italy (with Jeanne Wilmot Carter)
Not for Bread Alone: Writers on Food, Wine and the Art of Eating

HOLY FIRE

Nine Visionary Poets and the Quest for Enlightenment

Edited by

DANIEL HALPERN

HarperPerennial

A Division of HarperCollins*Publishers*

for Lily

The Dancer and the Dance

———————————————

Since this page cannot legibly accommodate all of the copyright notices for the individual works that are reprinted here, pages 329–330 constitute an extension of the copyright page.

HarperCollins books may be purchased for educational, business, or sales promotional use. For information please write: Special Markets Department, HarperCollins Publishers, Inc., 10 East 53rd Street, New York, NY 10022.

FIRST EDITION

Designed by Gloria Adelson/LuLu Graphics

Library of Congress Cataloging-in-Publication Data
    Holy fire : nine visionary poets and the quest for enlightenment /
    Daniel Halpern, editor.—1st ed.
      p. cm.
    ISBN 0-06-018240-7 / ISBN 0-06-098203-9 (pbk.)
    1. Poetry—Collections. 2. Visions—Poetry. 3. Imagination—Poetry.
  I. Halpern, Daniel, 1945–   .
  PN6101.H65 1994   94-11281
  808.81—dc20

94 95 96 97 98 CC/RRD 10 9 8 7 6 5 4 3 2 1
94 95 96 97 98 CC/RRD 10 9 8 7 6 5 4 3 2 1 (pbk.)

ACKNOWLEDGMENTS

The idea for an anthology of visionary poetry was initiated by the editors of the Quality Paperback Book Club, and so I wish to acknowledge their support and help: Andre Bernard, Tracy Brown, Kathy Kiernan, Linda Loewenthal, and David Rosen; I especially want to thank Alice Van Straalen, who seemed patient beyond Godot, who put so much of herself into this project, and allowed me to indulge myself in the visionary. Thanks too to my editor at HarperCollins, Charlotte Abbott, for reading this collection with clarity and intelligence.

I wish to thank Coleman Barks for his graceful and important translations of Rumi and Lalla—his devotion to their devotional work. And Jane Hirshfield for her translations of Lalla and Mirabai, as well as for her good advice and generosity. And Robert Bly—who has been a powerful force in American poetry in many ways for the past thirty years, not least of all as a tireless translator of poetry from around the world—for his Rumi and Mirabai versions.

A nod of appreciation also goes to the other translators in this volume, who have made the poetry of other languages accessible to English readers: to Andrew Shelling for his work on Mirabai; Louise Varèse, whose translations of Rimbaud many of us grew up with; and Stephen Mitchell, who has brought Rilke to contemporary readers with such sensitivity and brilliance. And I would like to acknowledge Alfred Kazin's work on *The Portable Blake*, which I used in making my selection from Blake's "The Four Zoas," as I did when I wrote a term paper on Blake's prophetic poems at Van Nuys High School back in 1963.

Finally, special thanks to Jeanne Wilmot Carter, who so carefully guided the assembling of this anthology.

D.H.

CONTENTS

LALLA

[Kashmir, 1320–1391]

Translated from the Kashmiri, Hindi, and Sanskrit by
Coleman Barks and Jane Hirshfield

Mirabai

[Northern India, ca. 1498–1550]

Translated from the Rajasthani by Andrew Shelling,
Robert Bly, and Jane Hirshfield

WILLIAM BLAKE

[England, 1757–1827]

Arthur Rimbaud

[France, 1854–1891]

Translated from the French by Louise Varèse

W. B. Yeats

[Ireland, 1865–1939]

RAINER MARIA RILKE

[Germany, 1875–1926]

Translated from the German by Stephen Mitchell

INTRODUCTION

I want to discuss in this brief introduction what visionary poetry, however defined, can be expected to produce. In preparing my selections I drew the boundaries lightly—in pencil, as it were—so as to cast as wide a net as possible over the poetic waters, in search of poems that do three things. First, they must honor their language (oral or written), whether it be English, French, German, Kashmiri, Hindi, Sanskrit, or Persian, acknowledging Santayana's observation that "the height of poetry is to speak the language of the gods." Second, the poems must fulfill, with unerring precision, the requirements of their form, whatever that form turns out to be. And third, the poetry must operate in a visionary realm—that is, present a view of the world that violates the superficial, reaches through the surface to touch the primal material. Wordsworth would call this act the seeing into the life of things; Ruskin wrote, "The greatest thing a human soul ever does in this world is to *see* something, and tell what it *saw* in a plain way. . . . To see clearly is poetry, prophecy, and religion,—all in one." What he was talking about is not the "seeing" of the representational; it is seeing with clarity the essential substance of the commonplace. Coleridge called it "armed vision," perception with the helping hand of a higher authority; Rimbaud believed that visionary poetry could be achieved by arriving at the unknown through the disordering of all the senses; and Blake, perhaps in most direct touch with the divine, wrote, "I am under the direction of Messengers from Heaven, Daily & Nightly."

I have selected for this volume those poets who *see* a world beyond their own. And poets who are comfortable with beatific and apocalyptic visions and ideas of transfiguration are poets who reimagine the cosmos. They imagine that they portray the Truth of existence, not simply "the facts." The poets in these pages are dancers and seers, singers and masters of the lyric, engravers, factory workers, princesses, saints, madmen, philosophers. For me, religious, spiritual, and devotional poetry, the poetry of the Romantics and the Symbolists, the work of the Metaphysical and the Beat poets, all enter the visionary domain.

These nine poets, who are representative of the visionary, have through a span of 700 years shared a dissatisfaction with the inherited zeitgeist; regardless of era, they have shared a sense that transcendence of the daily is not only possible but necessary to the discovery of Truth, a state that may require the creation of a new heaven and earth. Each poet leaps that chasm between the daily and the transcendent with a different repertoire of moves and styles. Some enjoy elation in heightened or transcendent psychological states, however induced; others achieve various forms of deep spiritual love and, directly or indirectly, affiliation or union with the Divine. To translate their visions for us, these poets have employed the lyric; they have relied on allegory, metaphor, and symbol to construct the objects of their perception, or *vision;* each has sung to us, and their poems have recorded their songs. Some of them look to the religious for substance, others to the prophetic, some pursue a universal unity; but all move forward transported via the visionary imagination. And it is, of course, the imagination that provides the instruments and energy necessary for the kind of transformation required of this poetry.

Poets inherit words handed down through the ages, voice to voice. In this way the poet is the vessel through which the enlightened material flows, flows through the valleys of allegory, metaphor, and symbol on the lyrical tide of the poet. The lyrical moment in poetry approaches the lasting timelessness of music, a moment that continually *comes around,* comes back, returns, and so, like music, is timeless and eternal—"All art aspires to the condition of music," Walter Pater said.

These are the gifts and the mandate of *all* true poets. However, visionary poets are bound to an additional task. They must believe they possess a proprietary interest in the imagination because the mandate of *their* poetry is not only to evoke human experience but to use their imagination to move beyond the confines of this experiential life in order to reenvision the world, perhaps even to create a better world. Which is to say, the visionary imagination is in the service of a higher order. The poet who wishes simply to document a moment in his life, in his century, on his street, accomplishes his lyrical transformation of the experience equally fueled by the fire of his imagination, yet without the burden of transcending his individual perception. These boundaries, as I suggested earlier, are easily transgressed, so that a poet normally outside the domain of the visionary can suddenly join the visionary company.

It is also useful to differentiate the visionary poet from the mystic. I would suggest that what the visionary poet can realize through his work goes beyond what the mystic can achieve. Emerson believed the mystic "nails a symbol to one sense, which was a true sense for a moment, but soon becomes old and false." The mystic, like the poet writing in a nonvisionary mode, is anchored (as in tethered) by culture and historical moment, whereas the visionary poet can escape the exigencies of his or her particular time and culture by invoking a world beyond the one we inhabit. It is only the poet working in the visionary mode who is equipped to provide the vision of the mystic everlastingness, because of his unique position on the crossbeam where poetry meets the mystical. Hence it is ironic that the visionary poet's task is very much dictated by an urgency endemic to the human condition: the need for Other-ness that has always drawn people into religion, that need to believe in a higher authority. Emerson wrote, "The religions of the world are the ejaculations of a few imaginative men."

Embarking upon the enviable job of assembling an anthology that gathers together poetry that could be called visionary, I did not worry overly about whether or not a particular poet has traditionally been categorized as visionary, because each of the poets represented here has reached into the fire, the holy fire of the soul, has been baptized by that flame and has emerged, via the poem; and through the imagination, each has been cleansed.

Randall Jarrell referred to the poet as one struck by lightness and touched by fire. It is my belief that each of the nine poets selected for this collection would satisfy Jarrell's poignant and poetic definition of the poet, as well as my notion of the visionary poet. *Holy Fire* begins with Rumi, Lalla, and Mirabai, who practiced out of the oral tradition in the thirteenth, fourteenth, and sixteenth centuries in Turkey, Kashmir, and India, respectively. The selection takes us next to William Blake and the British Isles in the eighteenth and nineteenth centuries. Then to the Continent—Rimbaud in nineteenth-century France and Rilke's early twentieth-century Germany—and to Yeats's turn-of-the-century Ireland. And finally to the New World, with Hart Crane representing the first half of this century and Allen Ginsberg bringing us to the living.

The choices were, as the anthologist's cliché goes, difficult ones. Each writer was selected because he or she represents something different in his or her role as poet. And although it is true that Mirabai and Lalla share psychic space, the affect of their work is quite different: whereas Mirabai is expansive and gregarious, Lalla is private, very much on her own mission; her work is tight and implosive, Mirabai is chatty and aggressive.

There are many poets who could (and should!) be here—a short list would certainly include Virgil and Dante; St. John of the Cross, Spenser, Milton, Smart, Coleridge, Hopkins, Baudelaire, Whitman, and Dickinson—a very short list. Although it is evident from reading my selections, it was also essential to my selection process that there be no suggestion of the poets having come out of similar traditions—in fact, quite the opposite. These poets share the visionary in the way planets share the sun. Moreover, none of these poets is *representative* of an age or moment in history. Each in his or her own way is anomalous, a radical, if you will, who broke from the mainstream, whatever it happened to be; they were not in their own time part of any visionary tradition. Perhaps in some irrational way there is a transgenerational logic to this fact, which relates to their unique ability to provide the vision of the mystic everlastingness without ties to history and culture. This said, Rumi, Lalla, and Mirabai did come out of a religious context and were part of an oral tradition; yet each was eager to divest himself or herself of *self*—Rumi merging with his friend Shams, Lalla and Mirabai with their respective lords, Shiva and the Dark One. Blake was so untouched by his contemporaries that he wasn't even considered a poet in his lifetime; Rimbaud was influenced by various styles, but finally he represents only himself. Truly, the poets in *Holy Fire* have invented themselves as poets and in no way would accept the possibility that they were part of a specific tradition.

I've selected some of the poets most obvious to my sense of the visionary, yet the argument is not over who is included but rather who is left out. Is it possible to complain about Blake or Yeats? *A Season in Hell* and *Illuminations* by Rimbaud or Rilke's *Duino Elegies*? Or the Sufi Rumi, and the inspirational Lalla and Mirabai? Even the less obvious—Hart Crane and Allen Ginsberg—seem in the context of the others to have a kind of inevitability; both envision a completed world fragmented in the one they inherited. More notable is the fact that I've left out poets such as Coleridge, Hopkins, Dickinson, and Whitman. For me the difficult decisions involved interesting issues; for example, I chose Ginsberg over Whitman for Ginsberg's attention to the hermetic, for the spirituality that runs through his work, for his attraction to Buddhist teachings, and for the ecstatic nature of his song, which ties him to Rumi, Lalla, and Mirabai. Certainly "Howl" was critical to the development of many poets writing today, a powerfully prophetic and incantatory piece of writing that appeared at a historic moment when the poetry community (readers and practitioners) knew what "Howl" meant and how to use it. This decision was also based on the relative familiarity of Whitman's poems. Ultimately, the choice seemed right, even daring, if I may say so—and, after all, this is a visionary anthology.

And I chose Crane over Hopkins not because I think he's a better poet, which I don't (and ranking bores me), but because the *texture* of his language, his impassioned writing and vision and uneqivocal evocation of industrialized America seem unique in American poetry. Did Emerson anticipate Crane when he wrote, "Yet America is a poem in our eyes; its ample geography dazzles the imagination, and it will not wait long for metres"? And, too, I like the way Crane and Ginsberg balance with Blake and Yeats—the unpredictable visionaries paired off against the prototypical.

*

It has been my goal to fill this volume with poets as disparate as Rumi, Lalla, Rimbaud, and Ginsberg, whose poems included here represent each at his or her best. I selected poems large in their encircling vision: Blake's "Visions of the Daughters of Albion," Rimbaud's "The Drunken Boat," Rilke's *Duino Elegies*, Yeats's "Sailing to Byzantium" and "The Tower," Crane's "The Bridge," and Ginsberg's "Howl." But I've also selected poems that address *aspects* of the larger vision, smaller parts of the overview. The works of Rumi, Lalla, and Mirabai invoke moments of a transfigured world, although, when each of their bodies of work is taken in its entirety, it certainly presents a completed vision.

However we feel about *what* the visionary poem is or is not, ultimately the poems in this collection attest to the power of the human imagination, its ability to transcend whatever obstacles the centuries toss to the street before us. This for me has been the visionary experience—to be guided and instructed, as Virgil revealed an unimaginable world to Dante, by the magical company of the poets who follow.

It is my hope that this collection of poems will blossom in the way the laurel twig blossomed in the hands of Swedenborg's angels when they affirmed a truth. The poets in these pages, through clarity of vision, raise the common and the plain to an enchanted, universal place, purified by holy fire—a landscape of the blessed, poems to celebrate the living.

DANIEL HALPERN

O sages standing in God's holy fire
As in the gold mosaic of a wall,
Come from the holy fire, perne in a gyre,
And be the singing-masters of my soul.
Consume my heart away; sick with desire
And fastened to a dying animal
It knows not what it is; and gather me
Into the artifice of eternity.

W. B. Yeats, "Sailing to Byzantium"

Your hand opens and closes and opens and closes.
If it were always a fist or always stretched open,
you would be paralyzed.

Your deepest presence is in every small contracting
        and expanding,
the two as beautifully balanced and coordinated
as bird wings.

Rumi, *Mathnawi*

And sometimes I have seen what men have thought
        they saw!

Arthur Rimbaud, "The Drunken Boat"

JELALUDDIN RUMI

The mystery does not get clearer by repeating
    the questions.
Nor is it bought with going to amazing places.
Until you've kept your eyes and your wanting
    still for fifty years
You don't begin to cross over from confusion.

"THE MYSTERY"

Jelaluddin Rumi

(Afghanistan/Turkey, 1207–1273)

Rumi was born in Balkh, in what today is Afghanistan, but early in his life his family was forced to flee the Mongol invasions. Stopping for a while in Nashapur, the family met the poet Attar, who was to become the first of Rumi's mentors. Attar identified the boy's special gifts and gave him the *Asrar Nama*—the *Book of Secrets*. In 1226 Rumi married and had a son.

But the critical moment in Rumi's life occurred at the age of thirty-seven, when he met a wandering dervish named Shams of Tabriz and his life changed dramatically. It is reported that Rumi's students, feeling threatened by Shams, stabbed him, although his body was never found. After his disappearance Rumi produced a prolific body of poetry, recorded in Persian—although Rumi himself did not actually *write* the poems down; they were collected as he recited them by his students or scribes. Before he died at the age of sixty-six, he had authored more than 3,000 lyrics and odes, as well as a six-volume poem of religious mysticism entitled the *Mathnawi*. His poetry attests to a life spent attempting to experience the divine by way of the mystical consciousness. Rumi is credited with founding the Malevi, the ecstatic dancing order we know as the Whirling Dervishes. The story goes that one day he was wandering in a bazaar when he heard the sound of goldsmiths hammering. Rumi burst into dance, whirling through the marketplace, and at that moment became the first "whirling dervish." According to Coleman Barks, the translator who has done much to make Rumi available to English readers, Shams himself spoke of Rumi as "ever-changing, always revealing a quality that hadn't been there before!" Furuzanfar, another contemporary, said that Rumi's eyes "flashed with a hypnotic brightness." After his meeting with Shams, Furuzanfar relates, Rumi abandoned his scholar's turban and gown for a smoke-colored turban and a robe of blue, a color which would signify his place in another world. Rumi was also known for his respect for all faiths—Muslim, Jewish, and Christian.

In describing the atmosphere of his poetry, Barks writes, "Rumi composes, with melting terms, a fluctuating music of presence and absence. His work becomes the clear, watery medium for a condition of incarnation: occasional ecstasy, continuous wonderment and longing, disconnections, union." Rumi is generally considered the greatest of the Sufi mystic poets.

For years, copying other people, I tried to know myself.
From within, I couldn't decide what to do.
Unable to see, I heard my name being called.
Then I walked outside.

WHEN THINGS ARE HEARD

The ear participates, and helps arrange marriages;
the eye has already made love with what it sees.

The eye knows pleasure, delights in the body's shape:
the ear hears words that talk about all this.

When hearing takes place, character areas change;
but when you see, inner areas change.

If all you know about fire is what you have heard
see if the fire will agree to cook you!

Certain energies come only when you burn.
If you long for belief, sit down in the fire!

When the ear receives subtly, it turns into an eye.
But if words do not reach the ear in the chest, nothing happens.

[TR. ROBERT BLY]

THE ELUSIVE ONES

They're lovers again: Sugar dissolving in milk.

Day and night, no difference. The sun *is* the moon:
an amalgam. Their gold and silver melt together.

This is the season when the dead branch and the green
branch are the same branch.

The cynic bites his finger because he can't understand.
Omar and Ali on the same throne,
two kings in one belt!

Nightmares fill with light like a holiday.
Men and angels speak one language.
The elusive ones finally meet.

The essence and evolving forms
run to meet each other like children
to their father and mother.

Good and evil, dead and alive, everything blooms
from one natural stem.

You know this already, I'll stop.
Any direction you turn it's one vision.

Shams, my body is a candle touched with fire.

THE JAR WITH THE DRY RIM

The mind is an ocean . . . and so many worlds
are rolling there, mysterious, dimly seen!
And our bodies? Our body is a cup, floating
on the ocean; soon it will fill, and sink . . .
Not even one bubble will show where it went down.

The spirit is so near that you can't see it!
But reach for it . . . don't be a jar
full of water, whose rim is always dry.
Don't be the rider who gallops all night
and never sees the horse that is beneath him.

[TR. ROBERT BLY]

I don't get tired of you. Don't grow weary
of being compassionate toward me!

All this thirst-equipment
must surely be *tired* of me,
the waterjar, the water-carrier.

I have a thirsty fish in me
that can never find enough
of what it's thirsty for!

Show me the way to the ocean!
Break these half-measures,
these small containers.

All this fantasy
and grief.

Let my house be drowned in the wave
that rose last night out of the courtyard
hidden in the center of my chest.

Joseph fell like the moon into my well.
The harvest I expected was washed away.
But no matter.

A fire has risen above my tombstone hat.
I don't want learning, or dignity,
or respectability.

I want this music and this dawn
and the warmth of your cheek against mine.

The grief-armies assemble,
but I'm not going with them.

This is how it always is
when I finish a poem.

A great silence overcomes me,
and I wonder why I ever thought
to use language.

[TR. ROBERT BLY]

Forget the world, and so
command the world.

Be a lamp, or a lifeboat, or a ladder.
Help someone's soul heal.
Walk out of your house like a shepherd.

Stay in the spiritual fire.
Let it cook you.

Be a well-baked loaf
and lord of the table.

Come and be served
to your brothers.

You have been a source of pain.
Now you'll be the delight.

You have been an unsafe house.
Now you'll be the one
who sees into the invisible.

I said this, and a voice came to my ear,
"If you become this, you will be *that*!"

Then silence,
and now more silence.

A mouth is not for talking.
A mouth is for tasting this sweetness.

Candle, wine, and friends,
on a Springlike night
in mid-December.

This love I have for you
makes everywhere I look
blaze up. The tip
of every feather burns.

A deep sweetness comes through sugarcane,
into the cut reed,
and now it's in the empty notes
of the flute.

Beheaded lovers don't complain.
They live hidden underground,
like people in lava cities.

There is no worse torture than knowing *intellectually*
about love and the way.

Those Egyptian women,
when they saw Joseph, were not *judging*
his handsomeness.

They were lost in it,
cutting their hands
as they cut their food.

Muhammed was completely empty
when he rose that night
through a hundred thousand years.

Let wind blow through us.
Let Shams cover
our shadows
like snow.

How does a part of the world leave the world?
How can wetness leave water?

Don't try to put out a fire
by throwing on more fire!
Don't wash a wound with blood!

No matter how fast you run,
your shadow more than keeps up.
Sometimes, it's in front!

Only full, overhead sun
diminishes your shadow.

But that shadow has been serving you!
What hurts you, blesses you.
Darkness is your candle.
Your boundaries are your quest.

I can explain this, but it would break
the glass cover on your heart,
and there's no fixing that.

You must have shadow and light-source both.
Listen, and lay your head under the tree of awe.

When from that tree, feathers and wings sprout
on you, be quieter than a dove.
Don't open your mouth for even a *cooooooo*.

When a frog slips into the water, the snake
cannot get it. Then the frog climbs back out
and croaks, and the snake moves toward him again.

Even if the frog learned to hiss, still the snake
would hear through the hiss the information
he needed, the frog-voice underneath.

But if the frog could be completely silent,
then the snake would go back to sleeping,
and the frog could reach the barley.

The soul lives there in the silent breath.
And that grain of barley is such that,
when you put it in the ground,
it grows.
         Are these enough words,
or shall I squeeze more juice from this?

Who am I, my Friend?

They say that Paradise will be perfect
with lots of clear white wine and all the beautiful women.
We hold on to times like this then,
since this is how it's going to be.

Think that you're gliding out from the face of a cliff
like an eagle. Think you're walking
like a tiger walks by himself in the forest.
You're most handsome when you're after food.

Spend less time with nightingales and peacocks.
One is just a voice, the other just a color.

THE NEW RULE

It's the old rule that drunks have to argue
and get into fights.
The lover is just as bad: He falls into a hole.
But down in that hole he finds something shining,
worth more than any amount of money or power.

Last night the moon came dropping its clothes in the street.
I took it as a sign to start singing,
falling *up* into the bowl of sky.
The bowl breaks. Everywhere is falling everywhere.
Nothing else to do.

Here's the new rule: Break the wineglass,
and fall toward the glassblower's breath.

How did you get away?
You were the pet falcon of an old woman.
Did you hear the falcon-drum?
You were a drunken songbird put in with owls.
Did you smell the odor of a garden?
You got tired of sour fermenting
and left the tavern.

You went like an arrow to the target
from the bow of time and place.
The man who stays at the cemetery pointed the way,
but you didn't go.
You became light and gave up wanting to be famous.
You don't worry about what you're going to eat,
so why buy an engraved belt?

I've heard of living at the center, but what about
leaving the center of the center?
Flying toward thankfulness, you become
the rare bird with one wing made of fear,
and one of hope. In autumn,
a rose crawling along the ground in the cold wind.
Rain on the roof runs down and out by the spout
as fast as it can.

Talking is pain. Lie down and rest,
now that you've found a friend to be with.

THE INDIAN PARROT

There was a merchant setting out for India.

He asked each male and female servant
what they wanted to be brought as a gift.

Each told him a different exotic object:
A piece of silk, a brass figurine,
a pearl necklace.

Then he asked his beautiful caged parrot,
the one with such a lovely voice,
and she said,
                "When you see the Indian parrots,
describe my cage. Say that I need guidance
here in my separation from them. Ask how
our friendship can continue with me so confined
and them flying about freely in the meadow mist.

Tell them that I remember well our mornings
moving together from tree to tree.

Tell them to drink one cup of ecstatic wine
in honor of me here in the dregs of my life.

Tell them that the sound of their quarreling
high in the trees would be sweeter
to hear than any music."

This parrot is the spirit-bird in all of us,
that part that wants to return to freedom,
and is the freedom. What she wants
from India is *herself*!

So this parrot gave her message to the merchant,
and when he reached India, he saw a field
full of parrots. He stopped
and called out what she had told him.

One of the nearest parrots shivered
and stiffened and fell down dead.
The merchant said, "This one is surely kin
to my parrot. I shouldn't have spoken."

He finished his trading and returned home
with the presents for his workers.

When he got to the parrot, she demanded her gift.
"What happened when you told my story
to the Indian parrots?"

"I'm afraid to say."
                            "Master, you must!"

"When I spoke your complaint to the field
of chattering parrots, it broke
one of their hearts.

She must have been a close companion,
or a relative, for when she heard about you
she grew quiet and trembled, and died."

As the caged parrot heard this, she herself
quivered and sank to the cage floor.

This merchant was a good man.
He grieved deeply for his parrot, murmuring
distracted phrases, self-contradictory—
cold, then loving—clear, then
murky with symbolism.

A drowning man reaches for anything!
The Friend loves this flailing about
better than any lying still.

The One who lives inside existence
stays constantly in motion,
and whatever you do, that king
watches through the window.

When the merchant threw the "dead" parrot
out of the cage, it spread its wings
and glided to a nearby tree!

The merchant suddenly understood the mystery.
"Sweet singer, what was in the message
that taught you this trick?"

"She told me that it was the charm
of my voice that kept me caged.
Give it up, and be released!"

The parrot told the merchant one or two more
spiritual truths. Then a tender goodbye.

"God protect you," said the merchant,
"as you go on your new way.
I hope to follow you!"

THE HOOPOE'S TALENT

Whenever a pavilion was pitched in the countryside
for Solomon, the birds would come
to pay their respects and talk with him.

Solomon understood bird-language.
There was no confused twittering
in his presence. Each species spoke
its call distinctly.

Being understood is such a joy!
When a person is with people
that he or she cannot confide in,
it's like being tied up.

And I don't mean a cultural kinship.
There are Indians and Turks who speak the same language.
There are Turks who don't understand each other.

I'm talking of those who are inside
the one love together.
                        So, the birds were asking Solomon
questions and telling him their special talents.
They all hoped that they would be asked
to stay in Solomon's presence.
It came the turn of the hoopoe.
                        "My king,
I have only one talent, but I hope
it will be helpful to you."
                        "Say it."
"When I fly to the highest point
of my ability and look down,

I can see then through the earth
to the water table.

I can see whether it's muddy with clay,
or clear, running through stone.

I can see where the springs are,
and where good wells may be dug."

Solomon replied, "You will make a fine companion
for my expeditions into the wilderness!"

The jealous crow couldn't stand it.
He yelled out,
                    "If hoopoe has such keen eyesight,
why did she not see the snare
that caught her once?"
                         "Good question," said Solomon.
"What about this, hoopoe?"
                               "My water-seeing talent
is a true one. And it's also true
that I have been blind to things
that have trapped me. There is a will
beyond my knowing that causes
both my blindness and my clairvoyance.
Crow doesn't acknowledge that."

The Question

One dervish to another, *What was your vision of God's presence?*
I haven't seen anything.
But for the sake of conversation, I'll tell you a story.

God's presence is there in front of me, a fire on the left,
a lovely stream on the right.
One group walks toward the fire, *into* the fire, another
toward the sweet flowing water.
No one knows which are blessed and which not.
Whoever walks into the fire appears suddenly in the stream.
A head goes under on the water surface, that head
pokes out of the fire.
Most people guard against going into the fire,
and so end up in it.
Those who love the water of pleasure and make it their
        devotion
are cheated with this reversal.
The trickery goes further.
The voice of the fire tells the *truth,* saying *I am not fire.*
I am fountainhead. Come into me and don't mind the sparks.

If you are a friend of God, fire is your water.
You should wish to have a hundred thousand sets of
        mothwings,
so you could burn them away, one set a night.
The moth sees light and goes into fire. You should see fire
and go toward light. Fire is what of God is world-consuming.
Water, world-protecting.
Somehow each gives the appearance of the other. To these eyes
        you have now

what looks like water burns. What looks like
fire is a great relief to be inside.
You've seen a magician make a bowl of rice
seem a dish full of tiny, live worms.
Before an assembly with one breath he made the floor swarm
with scorpions that weren't there.
How much more amazing God's tricks.
Generation after generation lies down, defeated, they think,
but they're like a woman underneath a man, circling him.

One molecule-mote-second thinking of God's reversal of
        comfort and pain
is better than any attending ritual. That splinter
of intelligence is substance.
The fire and water themselves:
Accidental, done with mirrors.

EAT! BREAD-BIRD

Being hungry is better
than the maladies that come
with satiety.

Subtlety and lightness
and being true to your devotion
are some of the advantages
of fasting.

A certain person is eating, and greatly
enjoying, a piece of mouldy bread.

Someone asks, "Do you really *like* that food?"

He replies, "When you fast for two days,
a piece of bread tastes like layered pastry.
If I deny my appetite just a little,
I can have halvah every meal."

But fasting is not for everyone,
only those few who become God's lions.

True hunger
is not easy to have,
when fodder is always being set
in front of you with the invitation,

Eat. You're not a waterbird
that eats air.

You're a bread-bird. Eat!

Dervish at the Door

A dervish knocked at a house
to ask for a piece of dry bread,
or moist, it didn't matter.

"This is not a bakery," said the owner.

"Might you have a bit of gristle then?"

"Does this look like a butchershop?"

"A little flour?"

"Do you hear a grinding-stone?"

"Some water?"

"This is not a well."

Whatever the dervish asked for,
the man made some tired joke,
and refused to give him anything.

Finally the dervish ran in the house,
lifted his robe, and squatted
as though to take a shit.

"Hey, hey!"

"Quiet, you sad man. A deserted place
is a fine spot to relieve one's self,
and since there's no living thing here,
or means of living, it needs fertilizing."

The dervish began his own list
of questions and answers.

"What kind of bird are you? Not a falcon,
trained for the royal hand. Not a peacock,
painted with everyone's eyes. Not a parrot,
that talks for sugar cubes. Not a nightingale,
that sings like someone in love.

Not a hoopoe bringing messages to Solomon,
or a stork that builds on a cliffside.

What exactly do you do?
You are no known species.

You haggle and make jokes
to keep what you own for yourself.

You have forgotten the one
who doesn't care about ownership,
who doesn't try to turn a profit
from every human exchange."

I have been tricked by flying too close
to what I thought I loved.

Now the candleflame is out, the wine spilled,
and the lovers have withdrawn
somewhere beyond my squinting.

The amount I thought I'd won, I've lost.
My prayer becomes bitter and all about blindness.

How wonderful it was to be for a while
with those who surrender.

Others only turn their faces one way,
then another, like pigeons in flight.

I have known pigeons who fly in a nowhere,
and birds that eat grainlessness,

and tailors who sew beautiful clothes
by tearing them to pieces.

Someone said, "there is no dervish, or if there is a dervish,
　　that dervish is not there."

Look at a candleflame in bright noon sunlight.
　　If you put cotton next to it, the cotton will burn,
　　　　but its light has become completely mixed
　　　　　　with the sun.

That candlelight you can't find is what's left of a dervish.

If you sprinkle one ounce of vinegar over
　　two hundred tons of sugar,
　　　　no one will ever taste the vinegar.

A deer faints in the paws of a lion. The deer becomes
　　another glazed expression on the face of the lion.

These are rough metaphors for what happens to the lover.

There's no one more openly irreverent than a lover. He, or she,
　　jumps up on the scale opposite eternity
　　　　and claims to balance it.

And no one more secretly reverent.

A grammar lesson: "The lover died."
　　"Lover" is subject and agent, but that can't be!
　　　　The "lover" is defunct.

Only grammatically is the dervish-lover a doer.

In reality, with he or she so overcome,
　　so dissolved into love,
　　　　all qualities of doing-ness
　　　　　　disappear.

There once was a sneering wife
who ate all her husband brought home
and lied about it.

One day it was some lamb for a guest
who was to come. He had worked two hundred days
in order to buy that meat.

When he was away, his wife cooked a kabob
and ate it all, with wine.

The husband returns with the guest.
"The cat has eaten the meat," she says.
"Buy more, if you have any money left!"

He asks a servant to bring the scales,
and the cat. The cat weighs three pounds.
"The meat was three pounds, one ounce.
If this is the cat, where is the meat?
If this is the meat, where is the cat?
Start looking for one or the other!"

If you have a body, where is the spirit?
If you're spirit, what is the body?

This is not our problem to worry about.
Both are both. Corn is corn-grain and cornstalk.
The divine butcher cuts us a piece from the thigh,
and a piece from the neck.

Invisible, visible, the world
does not work without both.

If you throw dust at someone's head, nothing will
        happen.
If you throw water, nothing.
But combine them into a lump. That marriage
of water and dirt cracks open the head,
and afterwards there are other marriages.

I need a mouth as wide as the sky
to say the nature of a True Person, language
as large as longing.

The fragile vial inside me often breaks.
No wonder I go mad and disappear for three days
every month with the moon.

For anyone in love with you,
it's always these invisible days.

I've lost the thread of the story I was telling.
My elephant roams his dream of Hindustan again.
Narrative, poetics, destroyed, my body,
a dissolving, a return.

Friend, I've shrunk to a hair trying to say your story.
Would you tell mine?
I've made up so many love stories.
Now I feel fictional.
Tell *me*!
The truth is, you are speaking, not me.
I am Sinai, and you are Moses walking there.
This poetry is an echo of what you say.
A piece of land can't speak, or know anything!
Or if it can, only within limits.

The body is a device to calculate
the astronomy of the spirit.
Look through that astrolabe
and become oceanic.

Why this distracted talk?
It's not my fault I rave.
You did this.
Do you approve of my love-madness?

Say yes.
What language will you say it in, Arabic or Persian,

or what? Once again, I must be tied up.
Bring the curly ropes of your hair.

Now I remember the story.
A True Man stares at his old shoes
and sheepskin jacket. Every day he goes up
to his attic to look at his work-shoes and worn-out coat.
This is his wisdom, to remember the original clay
and not get drunk with ego and arrogance.

To visit those shoes and jacket
is praise.

The Absolute works with nothing.
The workshop, the materials,
are what does not exist.

Try and be a sheet of paper with nothing on it.
Be a spot of ground where nothing is growing,
where something might be planted,
a seed, possibly, from the Absolute.

Someone who doesn't know the Tigris River exists
brings the Caliph who lives near the river
a jar of fresh water. The Caliph accepts, thanks him,
and gives in return a jar filled with gold coins.

"Since this man has come through the desert,
he should return by water." Taken out by another door,
the man steps into a waiting boat
and sees the wide freshwater of the Tigris.
He bows his head, "What wonderful kindness
that he took my gift."

Every object and being in the universe is
a jar overfilled with wisdom and beauty,
a drop of the Tigris that cannot be contained
by any skin. Every jarful spills and makes the earth
more shining, as though covered in satin.
If the man had seen even a tributary
of the great river, he wouldn't have brought
the innocence of his gift.

Those that stay and live by the Tigris
grow so ecstatic that they throw rocks at the jugs,
and the jugs become perfect!
                              They shatter.
The pieces dance, and water. . . .
                              Do you see?
Neither jar, nor water, nor stone,
                              nothing.

You knock at the door of Reality.
You shake your thought-wings, loosen
your shoulders,
                 and open.

We can't help being thirsty,
moving toward the voice
of water.
                Milk-drinkers draw close
to the mother. Muslims, Christians, Jews,
Buddhists, Hindus, shamans,
everyone hears the intelligent sound
and moves, with thirst, to meet it.

Clean your ears. Don't listen
for something you've heard before.

Invisible camel bells,
                slight footfalls in sand.

Almost in sight! The first word they call out
will be the last word of our last poem.

DESIRE AND THE IMPORTANCE
OF FAILING

A window opens.
A curtain pulls back.

The lamps of lovers connect,
not at their ceramic bases,
but in their lightedness.

No lover wants union with the Beloved
without the Beloved also wanting the lover.

Love makes the lover weak,
while the Beloved gets strong.

Lightning from here strikes *there*.
When you begin to love God, God
is loving *you*. A clapping sound
does not come from one hand.

A thirsty man calls out, "Delicious water,
where are you?" while the water moans,
"Where is the water-drinker?"

The thirst in our souls *is* the attraction
put out by the water itself.

We belong to it,
and it to us.

God's wisdom made us lovers of one another.
In fact, all the particles of the world
are in love and looking for lovers.

Pieces of straw tremble
in the presence of amber.
We tremble like iron filings
welcoming the magnet.

Whatever that presence gives us
we take in. Earth signs feed.
Water signs wash and freshen.
Air signs clear the atmosphere.
Fire signs jiggle the skillet,
so we cook without getting burnt.

And the Holy Spirit helps with everything,
like a young man trying to support a family.
We, like the man's young wife, stay home,
taking care of the house, nursing the children.

Spirit and matter work together like this,
in a division of labor.

Sweethearts kiss and taste the delight
before they slip into bed and mate.

The desire of each lover is
that the work of the other be perfected.
By this man-and-woman cooperation,
the world gets preserved.
Generation occurs.

Roses and blue arghawan flowers flower.
Night and day meet in a mutual hug.

So different, but they do love each other,
the day and the night, like family.

And without their mutual alternation
we would have no energy.

Every part of the cosmos draws toward its mate.
The ground keeps talking to the body,
saying, "Come back! It's better for you
down here where you came from."

The streamwater calls to the moisture in the body.
The fiery aether whispers to the body's heat,
"I am your origin. Come with me."

Seventy-two diseases are caused
by the various elements pulling inside the body.
Disease comes, and the organs
fall out of harmony.

We're like the four different birds,
that each had one leg tied in
with the other birds.

A flopping bouquet of birds!
Death releases the binding, and they fly off,
but before that, their pulling is our pain.

Consider how the soul must be,
in the midst of these tensions,
feeling its own exalted pull.

My longing is more profound.
These birds want the sweet green herbs
and the water running by.

I want the infinite! I want wisdom.
These birds want orchards and meadows
and vines with fruit on them.

I want a vast expansion.
They want profit and the security
of having enough food.

Remember what the soul wants,
because in that, eternity
is *wanting* our souls!

Which is the meaning of the text,
They love That, and That loves them.

If I keep on explaining this,
the *Mathnawi* will run to eighty volumes!

The gist is: whatever anyone seeks,
that is seeking the seeker.

No matter if it's animal,
or vegetable, or mineral.

Every bit of the universe
is filled with wanting,
and whatever any bit wants,
wants the wanter!

This subject must dissolve again.

Back to Sadri Jahan and the uneducated peasant
who loved him, so that gradually Sadri Jahan
loved the lowly man. But who really
attracted who, whoom, Huuuu?

Don't be presumptuous and say one or the other.
Close your lips. The mystery of loving
is God's sweetest secret.

Keep it. Bury it. Leave it here
where I leave it, drawn as I am
by the pull of the Puller
to something else.

You know how it is. Sometimes
we plan a trip to one place,
but something takes us to another.

When a horse is being broken, the trainer
pulls it in many different directions,
so the horse will come to know
what it is to be ridden.

The most beautiful and alert horse is one
completely attuned to the rider.

God fixes a passionate desire in you,
and then disappoints you.
God does that a hundred times!

God breaks the wings of one intention
and then gives you another,
cuts the rope of contriving,
so you'll remember your dependence.

But sometimes, your plans work out!
You feel fulfilled and in control.

That's because, if you were always failing,
you might give up. But remember,
it is by *failures* that lovers
stay aware of how they're loved.

Failure is the key
to the kingdom within.

Your prayer should be, "Break the legs
of what I want to happen. Humiliate
my desire. Eat me like candy.
It's spring, and finally
I have no will."

I was dead, then alive.
Weeping, then laughing.

The power of love came into me,
and I became fierce like a lion,
then tender like the evening star.

He said, "You're not mad enough.
You don't belong in this house."

I went wild and had to be tied up.
He said, "Still not wild enough
to stay with us!"

I broke through another layer
into joyfulness.

He said, "It's not enough."
I died.

He said, "You're a clever little man,
full of fantasy and doubting."

I plucked out my feathers and became a fool.
He said, "Now you're the candle
for this assembly."

But I'm no candle. Look!
I'm scattered smoke.

He said, "You are the sheikh, the guide."
But I'm not a teacher. I have no power.

He said, "You already have wings.
I cannot give you wings."

But I wanted *his* wings.
I felt like some flightless chicken.

Then new events said to me,
"Don't move. A sublime generosity
is coming toward you."

And old love said, "Stay with me."
I said, "I will."

You are the fountain of the sun's light.
I am a willow shadow on the ground.
You make my raggedness silky.

The soul at dawn is like darkened water
that slowly begins to say *Thank you, thank you.*

Then at sunset, again, Venus gradually
changes into the moon and then the whole nightsky.

This comes of smiling back
at your smile.

The chess master says nothing,
other than moving the silent chess piece.

That I am part of the ploys
of this game makes me
amazingly happy.

On the day I die, when I'm being
carried toward the grave, don't weep.

Don't say, "He's gone! He's gone!"
Death has nothing to do with going away.

The sun sets and the moon sets,
but they're not *gone*. Death
is a coming together.

The tomb *looks* like a prison,
but it's really release
into union.

The human seed goes down in the ground
like a bucket into the well where Joseph is.

It grows and comes up full
of some unimagined beauty.

Your mouth closes here
and immediately opens
with a shout of joy there.

THE VARIETY OF INTELLIGENCES
IN HUMAN BEINGS

As many kinds as might be marked on a vertical
from the ground to the highest point of the sky:

One intelligence is a steadily burning orb.
One a tiny meteor flickering in and out the atmosphere of
        Venus.
There is a lantern that looks drunken, barely lighted,
then flaring to the ceiling, blackening the wall.
There is a cold night star. Many sorts
of intelligent fire. One, green, translucent, plant-green.
One a pole moving out from behind an obscurity.

There's not one mind-form everywhere equal, as some have
        said,
but it is particular intelligences that distort Universal
Intelligence, the ones that use light to hunt with.
The Mind of the Whole does otherwise. It gets a glimpse
of a lovely hunt going on, where God
is Hunter and everything else the hunted. That Mind
sees and tries to quit hunting and completely
be prey. That's the difference.

There's no way to win from where you've gotten yourself.
The queen has your king in danger. When you move out of
        check,
she takes the rook. Contrive instead
to be near one who serves well.
Figure how to be delivered from your own figuring.
Try to lose. Don't do anything
for power or influence. Run into the mind's fire.

Play this game because you love, and the playing is love.
Beg and cry and come walking on your knees.
Thoughtful supplication won't help.
Joseph's brothers wept, but inside
they were tricky and jealous.

LALLA

Dance, Lalla, with nothing on
but air. Sing, Lalla,
wearing the sky.

Look at this glowing day! What clothes
could be so beautiful, or
more sacred?

Lalla

(Kashmir, 1320–1391)

Another poet in the oral tradition, Lalla composed her mystical poems in the old Kashmiri dialect, and they come to us via the collective memory in Kashmiri, Hindi, and Sanskrit. Lalla, which translates "darling" in her native language, is also known as Lalla-Vakyana, Lalleswari, Lalla Yogiswari (her name in Sanskrit), Lal Ded (Granny Lal), and Mai Lal Diddi. Evidently there are very few Kashmiri, Hindus, or Muslims not familiar with her proverbial sayings and wisdom. For a short time she was married, but Lalla soon left her traditional life to study with a Hindu teacher. It was during this time that she began to travel around the countryside, singing her songs and dancing as she went, in rags or without any clothes at all.

There are many apocryphal stories associated with Lalla, ranging from the humorous slice-of-life—she spent evenings with her wicked mother-in-law, who was in the habit of placing a stone underneath her rice so it would appear that she had a large portion of food—to the miraculous, such as the story of her encounter with the famous Islamic saint Sayyid 'Ali Hamadani, the man credited with helping convert Kashmir to Islam. While wandering naked she spotted Hamadani and intuited his holiness. She cried out, "I have seen a man!" and ran into a baker's shop, where she jumped into a blazing oven and was immediately consumed by the flames. When the saint came into the shop looking for her, she suddenly emerged from the oven dressed in an aura of the brilliant green of Paradise.

Coleman Barks, who translated all but one of the following poems, compared Lalla with Rumi in this way: "Where Rumi is extravagant, Lalla is spare. Where Rumi is exuberant, Lalla is cold-sober. Rumi is intricate; Lalla, simple. Rumi works within a group; Lalla walks alone. Rumi is caressingly affectionate; Lalla, severely clear. Rumi is the imagination in full flower, always moving. Lalla is the condensed code of the body, the rooted, breathing word." Lalla belonged to the Kashmir school of Yoga Saivism, although her poems—direct, focused, and uncluttered—suggest an eclectic approach to life and religion. She celebrated through Shiva, "the changeless," whom she believed to be the one reality, God. Her dancing, some have said, reflected the dance of Shiva himself.

The soul, like the moon,
is new, and always new again.

And I have seen the ocean
continuously creating.

Since I scoured my mind
and my body, I too, Lalla,
am new, each moment new.

My teacher told me one thing,
Live in the soul.

When that was so,
I began to go naked,
and dance.

Wear just enough clothes to keep warm.
Eat only enough to stop the hunger-pang.

And as for your mind, let it work
to recognize who you are,
and the Absolute, and that
this body will become food
for the forest crows.

Those with a knack for walking in air,
those who can cool a fire,
still a stream,
or get milk from a wooden cow,
they're street jugglers, nothing more.

Ascetics wander shrine to shrine,
looking for what can only come
from visiting the soul.

Study the mystery you embody.
When you look up from that,
the dub grass looks fresher
a little ways off, and even more
green farther on. Stay here.

Meditate within eternity.
Don't stay in the mind.

Your thoughts are like a child fretting
near its mother's breast, restless
and afraid, who with a little guidance,
can find the path of courage.

There are those sleeping who are awake,
and others awake who are sound asleep.

Some of those bathing in sacred pools
will never get clean.

And there are others
doing household chores
who are free of any action.

Let them throw their curses.
If inside, I am connected
to what's true, my soul
stays quiet and clear.

Do you think Shiva worries
what people say!

If a few ashes fall on a mirror,
use them to polish it.

Fame is water
carried in a basket.

Hold the wind in your fist,
or tie up an elephant
with one hair.

These are accomplishments
that will make you famous.

Men and women now, even the best,
can barely remember their past lives,

and as for the children, whose lives
are getting harder and harder,
what will they do?

A time is coming so deformed
and unnatural that pears and apples
will ripen with the apricots,

and a daughter and a mother
will leave the house every day
hand in hand to find new strangers
to lie down with.

Loosen the load of sweetness I'm carrying.
The sling-knot is biting into my shoulder.

This day has been so meaningless.
I feel I can't go on.

When I was with my teacher, I heard a truth
that hurt my heart like a blister,

the tender pain of seeing
something I loved as an illusion.

The flocks I tended are gone.
I am a shepherd without even a memory

of what that means, climbing this mountain.
I feel so lost.

This was my inward way, until I came
into the presence of a Moon, this new knowledge

of how likenesses unite. Good Friend,
everything is You. I see only God.

Now the delightful forms and motions
are transparent. I look through them

and see myself as the Absolute. And here's
the answer to the riddle of this dream:

You leave, so that we two
can do one dance.

They arrive and others arrive,
and then they go, and the others go.
Day and night, a constant traffic.

Where do they come from?
Where do they go?

Does it *mean* anything?
Nothing, nothing, nothing.

What understanding comes through reading?
I decided not to let books determine
my life, but only whatever helps dissolve
infatuation and sentimental longing.

The shrewdness of innate,
subtle intellect is a fox
who knows what I need.

I came to this birth and rebirth universe
and found the self-lighting light.

If someone dies, it's nothing to me,
and if I die, it's nothing to anyone.

It's good to die,
and good to live long.

Dying and giving birth go on
inside the one consciousness,
but most people misunderstand

the pure play of creative energy,
how inside that, those
are one event.

Lalla, you've wandered so many places
trying to find your husband!

Now at last, inside the walls
of this body-house, in the heart-shrine,
you discover where he lives.

The sun, the lowest chakra of action,
disappeared. Then the highest, the moon.

Absorbed in the infinite, my mind dissolved.
Where now have the earth and sky gone?

Are they hiding in the nothing
like friends on a walk?

Shiva is the horse.
Vishnu puts the saddle on.
Brahma adjusts the stirrup.

And there is that in you
that will recognize the rider
those are waiting on: the unobstructed
sound, the nothing without name,
or lineage, or form,

which is continually changing
into the Sound and the Dot
within a human being who is
That meditating inside That,

the Sound and the Dot,
which are one thing, alone,
and the rider who mounts to ride.

Some people abandon their homes.
Others abandon hermitages.

All this renunciation does nothing,
if you're not deeply conscious.

Day and night, be aware
with each breath,
and live there.

My teacher, you are God to me!
Tell me the inner meaning
of my two breathings,
the one warm, the other cool.

"In your pelvis near the navel is the source
of many motions called the sun,
the city of the bulb.

As your vitality rises from that sun,
it warms, and in your mouth it meets
the downward flow through the fontanelle
of your higher self, which is cool
and called the moon, or Shiva.

This rivering mixture feels,
by turns, warm and cool."

What is worship? Who *are* this man
and this woman bringing flowers?

What kinds of flowers should be brought,
and what streamwater poured over the images?

Real worship is done by the mind
(Let that be a man) and by the desire
(Let that be a woman). And let those two
choose what to sacrifice.

There is a liquid that can be released
from under the mask of the face,
a nectar which when it rushes down
gives discipline and strength.

Let that be your sacred pouring.
Let your worship song be silence.

I was passionate,
filled with longing,
I searched
far and wide.

But the day
that the Truthful One
found me,
I was at home.

[TR. JANE HIRSHFIELD]

Playfully, you hid from me.
All day I looked.

Then I discovered
I was you,

and the celebration
of That began.

MIRABAI

I simply wander the road of the sadhus, lost in
    my songs.
Never stealing,
injuring no one—
who can discredit me?
Do you think I'd step down from an elephant
to ride on the haunch of an ass?

Mirabai

(Northern India, ca. 1498–1550)

There is not a great deal of historical information about the life of Mirabai, although she is considered one of the most famous of the north Indian *bhakti* poets who, in a movement that pervaded much of India from the thirteenth to the seventeenth century, expressed a devotional, passionate love for a god. Her work was crucial to the renaissance of ecstatic religious life in northern India.

Mirabai's biography, apocryphal or not, is familiar throughout India. It is generally believed that she was born into a well-to-do Rajput family—indeed, born a princess—in the village of Merta near the city of Ajmer, more than 200 miles from New Delhi, in the region known as Rajasthan. In 1516 she married Bhoj Raj, the crown prince of Mewar. Five years later he died in battle, and Mirabai began to spend more and more of her time praying to Krishna and visiting and receiving *sadhus* (holy men). This was not considered appropriate behavior for an aristocratic woman, and both Ratan Singh, the brother-in-law who succeeded her husband, and Vikram Singh, who next ascended to the throne, intrigued against her.

Unaffected by their opposition, Mirabai became an open rebel, railing against everything conventional. Unlike most of the *bhakti*, who were from the lower castes, she rejected the traditional customs and privileged background that had provided her with an education in Sanskrit and the arts of archery, dance, and prosody. Mirabai developed into a beautifully fanatical devotee of the proud god Krishna, whom she found seductively elusive, and eventually she adopted the ways of a *sadhu* herself. Because she presented her work by singing it, using a number of ragas, or melodies, Mirabai's poems were not written down until well after her death, and some of them were altered in dialect or meaning by the singers who passed them on. Although scholars have found it difficult to confirm which of the many poems attributed to her are authentic, there appear to be about 200 in total. Mirabai danced or begged barefoot as she sang these poems of her great love for Krishna.

Mirabai was not seeking literary acclaim for her work, but some of her lyrics have been called among the greatest of Indian literature. Her intention was entirely devotional, and she suggested that in a previous life she had been a *gopi*, one of the famous cowgirls who left their families to follow Krishna when he was a mischievous young cowherd in Vrindavan. Among the many stories that circulate today about Mirabai, the most famous are those that relate the three attempts on her life, after she committed to the independent life of a wandering *sadhu*: the first with poison, the second with a poisonous snake concealed in a basket, and the third by way of a bed of iron spikes. She survived each but finally left to wander northwestern India in pursuit of her beloved god she called by an assortment of names: "the Dark One," "the Raven Colored"; Giradhar (or Giridhara), "Lifter of Mountains"; Manamohan, "Exchanger of Hearts"; Hari, "the abductor"—a god endowed, as you can see, with various abilities.

As John Stratton Hawley has written in his *Songs of the Saints of India*, "Whoever she was . . . she fired the imagination with her fearless defiance. In one respect she is revered as Krishna's spiritual wife, as quiet and humble and self-sacrificing as any woman could be expected to be in relation to her 'husband-god,' but in another sense she is celebrated as the kind of person who shattered complacencies wherever she went, particularly by making it clear that the world's conception of a woman's place is not always a place one wants to be. In both these aspects, and as the only one of her gender to have earned a place on the honor roll of north India *bhakti* saints, she exerts a fascination that none of her male counterparts can match."

We understand that eventually Mirabai's in-laws, interested in the power that had accrued to her, sent out a group to retrieve their now-famous runabout daughter-in-law. When they found her, she asked to be allowed to spend her last night in a temple with an image of her beloved Krishna. In the morning she had disappeared, leaving behind only her robe and hair.

It's True I Went to the Market

My friend, I went to the market and bought the Dark One.
You claim by night, I claim by day.
Actually I was beating a drum all the time I was buying him.
You say I gave too much; I say too little.
Actually I put him on a scale before I bought him.
What I paid was my social body, my town body, my family
      body, and all my inherited jewels.
Mirabai says: The Dark One is my husband now.
Be with me when I lie down; you promised me this in an earlier
      life.

[Tr. Robert Bly]

Don't Go, Don't Go

Don't go, don't go. I touch your soles. I'm sold to you.
No one knows where to find the bhakti path, show me where to
      go.
I would like my own body to turn into a heap of incense and
      sandalwood and you set a torch to it.
When I've fallen down to gray ashes, smear me on your
      shoulders and chest.
Mira says: You who lift the mountains, I have some light, I want
      to mingle it with yours.

[Tr. Robert Bly]

ALL I WAS DOING WAS BREATHING

Something has reached out and taken in the beams of my eyes.
There is a longing, it is for his body, for every hair of that dark
 body.
All I was doing was being, and the Dancing Energy came by my
 house.
His face looks curiously like the moon, I saw it from the side,
 smiling.
My family says: "Don't ever see him again!" And imply things
 in a low voice.
But my eyes have their own life; they laugh at rules, and know
 whose they are.
I believe I can bear on my shoulders whatever you want to say
 of me.
Mira says: Without the energy that lifts mountains, how am I to
 live?

[TR. ROBERT BLY]

WHY MIRA CAN'T GO BACK TO HER OLD HOUSE

The colors of the Dark One have penetrated Mira's body; all the
      other colors washed out.
Making love with the Dark One and eating little, those are my
      pearls and my carnelians.
Meditation beads and the forehead streak, those are my scarves
      and my rings.
That's enough feminine wiles for me. My teacher taught me
      this.
Approve me or disapprove me: I praise the Mountain Energy
      night and day.
I take the path that ecstatic human beings have taken for
      centuries.
I don't steal money, I don't hit anyone. What will you charge
      me with?
I have felt the swaying of the elephant's shoulders; and now
      you want me to climb on a jackass? Try to be serious.

[TR. ROBERT BLY]

Binding my ankles with silver
I danced—
people in town called me crazy.
She'll ruin the clan,
said my mother-in-law,
and the prince
had a cup of venom delivered.
I laughed as I drank it.
Can't they see?—
body and mind aren't something to lose,
the Dark One's already seized them.
Mira's lord can lift mountains,
he is her refuge.

Sister, the Dark One won't speak to me.
Why does this useless body keep breathing?
Another night gone—
and no one's lifted my gown.
He won't speak to me.
Years pass, not a gesture.
They told me
he'd come when the rains came,
but lightning pierces the clouds,
the clock ticks until daybreak
and I feel the old dread.
Slave to the Dark One,
Mira's whole life is a long
        night of craving.

I am your slave.
Bind me in tethers, Mira's your slave.
She wakes up at dawn,
sits in the garden,
haunts the pathways of Vrindavan forest
making up ballads.
Fever, memory, craving—
birth after birth they trail after me—
I put on my saffron robe,
hoping to see you.
Yogins come to Vrindavan to know oneness,
hermits perform terrible spells,
holy men come to sing gospels—
but Mira is deeper, Lord,
and more secret.
She waits with a ruined heart every night
by the river
just for a glimpse.

He has stained me,
the color of raven he's stained me.
Beating a clay
two-headed drum at both ends
like a nautch girl I dance
before sadhus.
Back in town I'm called crazy,
drunkard, a love slut—
they incited the prince,
who ordered me poisoned,
but I drained the cup without missing a step.
Mira's lord is the true prince;
he stained her the color of raven.
Birth after birth
she is his.

Down by the river a flute!
O ruined heart,
what is conviction
that a flute player dissolves it?
Dark waters, dark trousers,
and Krishna darker than ever—
one bamboo flute note
so pure it drives Mira out of her mind.
Lord, this stumbling body,
        free it from torment—

Life on this planet is fragile,
why take up a burden?
From mother and father
come birth,
but from the font of creation comes karma.
People waste life,
heaping up merit like they're buying and selling—
it's pointless.
I sing out the raptures
of Hari, go into passions with sadhus,
nothing disturbs me.
Mira says: It's your power, Dark One—
but I'm the one
who crosses the limits.

My Dark One,
they've placed him off limits—
but I won't live without him.
Delighting in Hari,
coming and going with sadhus,
I wander beyond reach of the world's snare.
Body is wealth
but I give it away—
my head was long ago taken.
Full of rapture,
Mira flees the jabbering townsfolk—
going for refuge
to what cannot perish,
her Dark One.

Friend,
though the world sleeps,
the abandoned go sleepless.
From inside the palace
at a window, counting the planets,
someone threads teardrops onto a necklace.
The abandoned go sleepless.
Night has suddenly
vanished and Mira,
Mira has missed the hour of pleasure,
missed the Dark One who
strips her of pain.

Dark One,
all I request is a portion of love.
Whatever my defects,
you are for me an ocean of raptures.
Let the world cast its judgments
nothing changes my heart—
a single word from your lips is sufficient—
birth after birth
begging a share of that love.
Mira says: Dark One—enter the penetralia,
you've taken
this girl past the limits.

Guide this little boat
over the waters,
what can I give you for fare?
Our mutable world holds nothing but grief,
bear me away from it.
Eight bonds of karma
have gripped me—
the whole of creation
swirls through eight million wombs,
through eight million birth-forms we flicker.
Mira cries: Dark One—
take this little boat to the far shore,
put an end to coming
and going.

Thick overhead
clouds of the monsoon,
a delight to this feverish heart.
Season of rain,
season of uncontrolled whispers—the Dark One's returning!
O swollen heart,
O sky brimming with moisture—
tongued lightning first
and then thunder,
convulsive spatters of rain
and then wind, chasing the summertime heat.
Mira says: Dark One,
I've waited—
it's time to take my songs
into the street.

Why life,
why again,
and what reason birth as a woman?
Good deeds in former lives, they say.
But—
growth, cut, cut, decay—
life disappears second by second
and never comes back,
a leaf torn from its branch
goes twirling away.
Look at this raging ocean of life forms,
swift, unappeasable—
everything caught in its tide.
O beloved, take this raft quickly
and lead it to shore.

This is the seal of
dark love—
that my eyes should thrill with a vision.
My friend, I put on a bride's ornamentation
that my lover come quickly.
I've chosen no
desolate man
who comes to birth only to perish—
O unbreakable gem,
I take the Dark One to bed!
He sates Mira's passion,
life after life
she awaits his arrival.

Friend, I see
only the Dark One—
a dark swelling,
dark luster,
I'm fixed in trances of darkness.
Wherever my feet
touch soil I am dancing—
Oh Mira sees into the darkness,
she ambles the back
country roads.

Ten thousand thanks
O astrologer
for announcing the Dark One's arrival!
Dizzy, ecstatic,
my soul goes into her bedroom.
Five companions converge,
five senses,
to give him unparalleled pleasure.
One glimpse of his form
dispels anguish—
all my erotic longings bear fruit.
Shyam, the ocean of pleasure
has come into me.

The plums tasted
sweet to the unlettered desert-tribe girl—
but what manners! To chew into each!
She was ungainly,
low-caste, ill mannered and dirty,
but the god took the
fruit she'd been sucking.
Why? She knew how to love.
She might not distinguish
splendor from filth
but she'd tasted the nectar of passion.
Might not know any Veda,
but a chariot swept her away—
now she frolics in heaven, ecstatically bound to her god.
The Lord of Fallen Fools, says Mira,
will save anyone
who can practice rapture like that—
I myself in a previous birth
was a cowherding girl
at Gokul.

Yogin, I did not touch
your intimate secret.
Taking a mystical posture, I sat
in a cave,
beads at my throat, my limbs pasted with ash.
I had raptures over the Dark One, but no—
I never touched
his imperishable secret—
what Mira obtains
has been written by fate.

In my dream, sister,
the Lord of the Downtrodden wed me.
Deities danced in attendance,
fifty-six million.
The Dark One was groom in my dream.
In my dream were arched marriage gateways,
a clasping of hands, sister.
In a dream
the Lord of the Downtrodden
married Mira and took her to bed—
good fortune from previous births
bears its fruit.

Refuge in you, Dark One—
you alone
know how to save me.
A girl possessed,
I shamble through the sixty-eight places
of pilgrimage
but haven't the wit to know failure.
Hear my cry, O Murari—
nothing on earth
looks like it's "mine."
Mira gave you her trust, now it's your move—
spring her from this noose
    we call "world."

Hear my plea, Dark One, I am
your servant—
a vision of you has driven me mad,
separation eats at my limbs.
Because of you
I'll become a yogini and ramble
from city to city
scouring the hidden quarters—
pasted with ash, clad in a deerskin,
my body wasting
to cinder.
I'll circle from forest to forest,
wretched and howling—
O Unborn, Indestructible,
come to your beggar!
Finish her pain and touch her
with pleasure!
This coming and going will end,
says Mira,
with me clasping your
    feet forever.

Dark One,
how can I sleep?
Since you left my bed
the seconds drag past like epochs,
each moment
a new torrent of pain.
I am no wife,
no lover comes through the darkness—
lamps, houses, no comfort.
On my couch
the embroidered flowers
pierce me like thistles,
    I toss through the night.

Yet who would believe my story?
That a lover
bit my hand like a snake,
and the venom bursts through
    and I'm dying?

I hear
the peacock's faraway gospel,
the nightingale's love song,
the cuckoo—
thickness on thickness folds through the sky,
clouds flash with rain.
Dark One, is there no love
in this world
that such anguish continues?
Mira waits for a single
    glance from your eye.

When can I meet
the Dark Lord?
Fifteen hours a day
caught up in duties,
nine more absent in sleep.
Human birth, says Mira,
is precious
but we get it and waste it in slumber.
Give yourself to the Dark One—
fate never swerves
        from its course.

Why this impulse
to hurt me, O cuckoo?
I was in my own
hut asleep
when you cried out a love song—
rubbing salt in the wound.
There you sat,
high on a tree branch,
singing from deep
        in your throat—

THE HEAT OF MIDNIGHT TEARS

Listen, my friend, this road is the heart opening,
kissing his feet, resistance broken, tears all night.

If we could reach the Lord through immersion in water,
I would have asked to be born a fish in this life.
If we could reach Him through nothing but berries and wild
  nuts
then surely the saints would have been monkeys when they
    came from the womb!
If we could reach him by munching lettuce and dry leaves
then the goats would surely get to the Holy One before us!

If the worship of stone statues could bring us all the way,
I would have adored a granite mountain years ago.

Mirabai says, "The heat of midnight tears will bring you to
    God."

[TR. ROBERT BLY]

Unbreakable, O Lord,
Is the love
That binds me to You:
Like a diamond,
It breaks the hammer that strikes it.

My heart goes into You
As the polish goes into the gold.
As the lotus lives in its water,
I live in You.

Like the bird
That gazes all night
At the passing moon,
I have lost myself dwelling in You.

O my Beloved—
Return.

[TR. JANE HIRSHFIELD]

My Beloved is lovely to look at,
Sweet to taste.

His is the Breath inside the breath,
His eyes uphold all Creation,
His soul is the Soul.

The daily world is false,
Its people are false,
All that we see is empty.

What we call husband,
What we call wife, is false.

If the King calls me wife,
He spits on my Husband,
My one true Bridegroom,
Who sits on the throne of the World.

I cast off silk dresses and gold,
And delight in wearing His garland.

I put His mark on my forehead,
And live with His saints.

His lotus feet are my only home.

Mira says,
To be human and not know the Lord
Is truly the womb of sorrow.

[TR. JANE HIRSHFIELD]

To be born in this human body is rare.
Do not throw away
The reward of your past good deeds.

Life passes in an instant,
The leaf will never go back to the branch,
The ocean of transmigration is wide.

Giridhara, your Name
Is the boat that holds us as we cross.
Take me quickly.

With Mira,
All the enlightened ones sing
The same words,
Crossing that tide:

"Awaken and sleep no more—
Brief are the days of life."

[Tr. Jane Hirshfield]

O my friends,
What can you tell me of Love,
Whose pathways are filled with strangeness?
When you offer the Great One your love,
At the first step your body is crushed.
Next be ready to offer your head as his seat.
Be ready to orbit his lamp like a moth giving in to the light,
To live in the deer as she runs toward the hunter's call,
In the partridge that swallows hot coals for love of the moon,
In the fish that, kept from the sea, happily dies.
Like a bee trapped for life in the closing of the sweet flower,
Mira has offered herself to her Lord.
She says, the single Lotus will swallow you whole.

[TR. JANE HIRSHFIELD]

Love has stained my body
To the color of the One Who Holds Up Mountains.
When I dressed in the world's five fabrics,
I only played hide and seek—
For disguised though I was, the Lifting One caught me.
And seeing his beauty, I offered Him all that I am.
Friends, let those whose Beloved is absent write letters—
Mine dwells in the heart, and neither enters nor leaves.
Mira has given herself to her Lord Giridhara.
Day or night, she waits only on Him.

[TR. JANE HIRSHFIELD]

O friends, I am mad
With love, and no one sees.

My mattress is a sword-point,
How can I sleep
When the bed of my Beloved
Is spread open elsewhere?

Only those who have felt the knife
Can understand the wound,
Only the jeweller
Knows the nature of the jewel.

I have lost it,
That anguish takes me from door to door,
But no doctor answers.

Mira calls her Lord: O Dark One,
Only You can heal this pain.

[Tr. Jane Hirshfield]

Drunk, turbulent clouds
roll overhead
but they bring from the Dark One
no message.
Listen—
the cry of a peacock,
a nightingale's faraway ballad,
a cuckoo.
Lightning
flares in the darkness,
a rejected girl shivers,
thunder, sweet wind and rain.
Lifetimes ago
Mira's heart went with the Dark One—
tonight in her solitude
infidelity spits
    like a snake—

WILLIAM BLAKE

He who binds to himself a joy
Does the winged life destroy;
But he who kisses the joy as it flies
Lives in eternity's sun rise.

"ETERNITY"

William Blake

(England, 1757–1827)

It is interesting to note that William Blake, a master engraver and illustrator of books, during his own lifetime was barely thought of as a poet. And for nearly half a century after his death, he was basically a forgotten poet. While alive he was considered a slightly odd eccentric, if not a downright madman. Wordsworth wrote of him, "There is no doubt this poor man was mad, but there is something in the madness of this man which interests me more than the sanity of Lord Byron and Walter Scott."

Blake's artistic gifts manifested themselves early. As a young boy he was sent to be an apprentice to an engraver, and following that he enrolled in the Royal Academy. His visions crowded in on him at an early age, too. Before turning ten he saw an angel-filled tree on Peckham Rye. His first collection of poems, *Poetical Sketches*, published in 1783, was unillustrated text, but after that almost all his literary work was conceived in combination with his own design and illustrations.

When his brother Robert died, Blake saw Robert's beloved spirit ascend heavenward, "clapping its hands for joy." We are to understand that it was his brother's spirit who later returned to reveal the etching process by which in 1789 Blake produced the luminous illustrations for the startlingly pure poems of *Songs of Innocence*.

Blake's actual physical presence had a strong impact, too—upon meeting him for the first time, his wife, Catherine, whom he married in 1782, was so overwhelmed that she had to withdraw from him until she regained her composure. Although initially he shared his generation's enthusiasm for what he expected to be the cultural change brought on by the French Revolution, Blake's vision was totally singular, and would be elaborated in a private mythology that became increasingly complex. This symbolic process deepened in 1794 with *The Book of Urizen* and continued in, among other works, *The Song of Los*, *The Book of Ahania*, and *The Book of Los*. These works consider the cosmos, exploring the nature of good and evil, the oppression of traditional morality, and the importance of creativity in confronting the stagnation of society. The later works—*Milton* and *Jerusalem* among them—show the influence of Christianity and are symbolic in nature, intended to match the Bible for visionary and spiritual impact.

Ironically, because Blake printed and illustrated his books of poems himself in beautifully produced editions, very few copies of his collections were available for distribution. For a time William Hayley, a country gentleman, found a house in rural Felpham for Blake and his wife, as well as some commissions for the poet. But even the sympathetic Hayley, like so many others, failed to understand the nature of Blake's genius and ended up oppressing the poet with his personal notions instead of freeing Blake to pursue his gifts. Back in London, Blake made several efforts to earn some income from his painting, but his exhibits languished as a result of misunderstanding of the work and skepticism about its creator.

In his later years Blake finally found himself in a small circle of appreciative friends—disciples, nearly—who were in awe of his genius; some would even stay up with him as he received his nocturnal spirit visitors. Because of the way his poems anticipated the nature of the modern world, Stanley Kunitz wrote of him, "It could be argued that he dared . . . to be the first modern poet." Certainly when the issue of visionary poetry is raised, Blake is the first poet in the modern tradition who comes to mind. Blake wrote to a friend, "I am not ashamed, afraid, or averse to tell you what Ought to be Told. That I am under the direction of Messengers from Heaven, Daily & Nightly." It was his mission to produce one of the greatest bodies of poetry of any century. Blake was a champion of the imagination; if Rumi, Lalla, and Mirabai believed in the reality of God, Blake believed in the reality and transformative powers of the imagination.

from SONGS OF INNOCENCE

INTRODUCTION

Piping down the valleys wild,
Piping songs of pleasant glee,
On a cloud I saw a child,
And he laughing said to me:

"Pipe a song about a Lamb!"
So I piped with merry chear.
"Piper, pipe that song again;"
So I piped: he wept to hear.

"Drop thy pipe, thy happy pipe;
Sing thy songs of happy chear:"
So I sung the same again,
While he wept with joy to hear.

"Piper, sit thee down and write
In a book, that all may read."
So he vanish'd from my sight,
And I pluck'd a hollow reed,

And I made a rural pen,
And I stain'd the water clear,
And I wrote my happy songs
Every child may joy to hear.

THE ECCHOING GREEN

The Sun does arise,
And make happy the skies;
The merry bells ring
To welcome the Spring;
The skylark and thrush,
The birds of the bush,
Sing louder around
To the bells' chearful sound,
While our sports shall be seen
On the Ecchoing Green.

Old John, with white hair,
Does laugh away care,
Sitting under the oak,
Among the old folk.
They laugh at our play,
And soon they all say:
"Such, such were the joys
When we all, girls & boys,
In our youth time were seen
On the Ecchoing Green."

Till the little ones, weary,
No more can be merry;
The sun does descend,
And our sports have an end.
Round the laps of their mothers
Many sisters and brothers,
Like birds in their nest,
Are ready for rest,
And sport no more seen
On the darkening Green.

THE LITTLE BLACK BOY

My mother bore me in the southern wild,
And I am black, but O! my soul is white;
White as an angel is the English child,
But I am black, as if bereav'd of light.

My mother taught me underneath a tree,
And sitting down before the heat of day,
She took me on her lap and kissed me,
And pointing to the east, began to say:

"Look on the rising sun: there God does live,
And gives his light, and gives his heat away;
And flowers and trees and beasts and man receive
Comfort in morning, joy in the noonday.

"And we are put on earth a little space,
That we may learn to bear the beams of love;
And these black bodies and this sunburnt face
Is but a cloud, and like a shady grove.

"For when our souls have learn'd that heat to bear,
The cloud will vanish; we shall hear his voice,
Saying: 'Come out from the grove, my love & care,
And round my golden tent like lambs rejoice.' "

Thus did my mother say, and kissed me;
And thus I say to little English boy:
When I from black and he from white cloud free,
And round the tent of God like lambs we joy,

I'll shade him from the heat, till he can bear
To lean in joy upon our father's knee;
And then I'll stand and stroke his silver hair,
And be like him, and he will then love me.

THE CHIMNEY SWEEPER

When my mother died I was very young,
And my father sold me while yet my tongue
Could scarcely cry " 'weep! 'weep! 'weep! 'weep!"
So your chimneys I sweep, & in soot I sleep.

There's little Tom Dacre, who cried when his head,
That curl'd like a lamb's back, was shav'd: so I said
"Hush, Tom! never mind it, for when your head's bare
You know that the soot cannot spoil your white hair."

And so he was quiet, & that very night,
As Tom was a-sleeping, he had such a sight!
That thousands of sweepers, Dick, Joe, Ned, & Jack,
Were all of them lock'd up in coffins of black.

And by came an Angel who had a bright key,
And he open'd the coffins & set them all free;
Then down a green plain leaping, laughing, they run,
And wash in a river, and shine in the Sun.

Then naked & white, all their bags left behind,
They rise upon clouds and sport in the wind;
And the Angel told Tom, if he'd be a good boy,
He'd have God for his father, & never want joy.

And so Tom awoke; and we rose in the dark,
And got with our bags & our brushes to work.
Tho' the morning was cold, Tom was happy & warm;
So if all do their duty they need not fear harm.

LAUGHING SONG

When the green woods laugh with the voice of joy,
And the dimpling stream runs laughing by;
When the air does laugh with our merry wit,
And the green hill laughs with the noise of it;

When the meadows laugh with lively green,
And the grasshopper laughs in the merry scene,
When Mary and Susan and Emily
With their sweet round mouths sing "Ha, Ha, He!"

When the painted birds laugh in the shade,
Where our table with cherries and nuts is spread,
Come live & be merry, and join with me,
To sing the sweet chorus of "Ha, Ha, He!"

THE DIVINE IMAGE

To Mercy, Pity, Peace, and Love
All pray in their distress;
And to these virtues of delight
Return their thankfulness.

For Mercy, Pity, Peace, and Love
Is God, our father dear,
And Mercy, Pity, Peace, and Love
Is Man, his child and care.

For Mercy has a human heart,
Pity a human face,
And Love, the human form divine,
And Peace, the human dress.

Then every man, of every clime,
That prays in his distress,
Prays to the human form divine,
Love, Mercy, Pity, Peace.

And all must love the human form,
In heathen, turk, or jew;
Where Mercy, Love, & Pity dwell
There God is dwelling too.

HOLY THURSDAY

'Twas on a Holy Thursday, their innocent faces clean,
The children walking two & two, in red & blue & green,
Grey-headed beadles walk'd before, with wands as white as
      snow,
Till into the high dome of Paul's they like Thames' waters flow.

O what a multitude they seem'd, these flowers of London town!
Seated in companies they sit with radiance all their own.
The hum of multitudes was there, but multitudes of lambs,
Thousands of little boys & girls raising their innocent hands.

Now like a mighty wind they raise to heaven the voice of song,
Or like harmonious thunderings the seats of Heaven among.
Beneath them sit the aged men, wise guardians of the poor;
Then cherish pity, lest you drive an angel from your door.

William Blake   93

NIGHT

The sun descending in the west,
The evening star does shine;
The birds are silent in their nest,
And I must seek for mine.
The moon like a flower
In heaven's high bower,
With silent delight
Sits and smiles on the night.

Farewell, green fields and happy groves,
Where flocks have took delight.
Where lambs have nibbled, silent moves
The feet of angels bright;
Unseen they pour blessing
And joy without ceasing,
On each bud and blossom,
And each sleeping bosom.

They look in every thoughtless nest,
Where birds are cover'd warm;
They visit caves of every beast,
To keep them all from harm.
If they see any weeping
That should have been sleeping,
They pour sleep on their head,
And sit down by their bed.

When wolves and tygers howl for prey,
They pitying stand and weep;
Seeking to drive their thirst away,
And keep them from the sheep;

But if they rush dreadful,
The angels, most heedful,
Receive each mild spirit,
New worlds to inherit.

And there the lion's ruddy eyes
Shall flow with tears of gold,
And pitying the tender cries,
And walking round the fold,
Saying "Wrath, by his meekness,
And by his health, sickness
Is driven away
From our immortal day.

"And now beside thee, bleating lamb,
I can lie down and sleep;
Or think on him who bore thy name,
Graze after thee and weep.
For, wash'd in life's river,
My bright mane for ever
Shall shine like the gold
As I guard o'er the fold."

NURSE'S SONG

When the voices of children are heard on the green
And laughing is heard on the hill,
My heart is at rest within my breast
    And everything else is still.

"Then come home, my children, the sun is gone down
And the dews of night arise;
Come, come, leave off play, and let us away
Till the morning appears in the skies."

"No, no, let us play, for it is yet day
And we cannot go to sleep;
Besides, in the sky the little birds fly
And the hills are all cover'd with sheep."

"Well, well, go & play till the light fades away
And then go home to bed."
The little ones leaped & shouted & laugh'd
    And all the hills ecchoed.

A Dream

Once a dream did weave a shade
O'er my Angel-guarded bed,
That an Emmet lost its way
Where on grass methought I lay.

Troubled, 'wilder'd, and forlorn,
Dark, benighted, travel-worn,
Over many a tangled spray,
All heart-broke I heard her say:

"O, my children! do they cry?
Do they hear their father sigh?
Now they look abroad to see:
Now return and weep for me."

Pitying, I drop'd a tear;
But I saw a glow-worm near,
Who replied: "What wailing wight
Calls the watchman of the night?

"I am set to light the ground,
While the beetle goes his round:
Follow now the beetle's hum;
Little wanderer, hie thee home."

from SONGS OF EXPERIENCE

THE TYGER

Tyger! Tyger! burning bright
In the forests of the night,
What immortal hand or eye
Could frame thy fearful symmetry?

In what distant deeps or skies
Burnt the fire of thine eyes?
On what wings dare he aspire?
What the hand dare sieze the fire?

And what shoulder, & what art,
Could twist the sinews of thy heart?
And when thy heart began to beat,
What dread hand? & what dread feet?

What the hammer? what the chain?
In what furnace was thy brain?
What the anvil? what dread grasp
Dare its deadly terrors clasp?

When the stars threw down their spears,
And water'd heaven with their tears,
Did he smile his work to see?
Did he who made the Lamb make thee?

Tyger! Tyger! burning bright
In the forests of the night,
What immortal hand or eye
Could frame thy fearful symmetry?

MY PRETTY ROSE-TREE

A flower was offer'd to me,
Such a flower as May never bore;
But I said "I've a Pretty Rose-tree,"
And I passed the sweet flower o'er.

Then I went to my Pretty Rose-tree,
To tend her by day and by night;
But my Rose turn'd away with jealousy,
And her thorns were my only delight.

LONDON

I wander thro' each charter'd street,
Near where the charter'd Thames does flow,
And mark in every face I meet
Marks of weakness, marks of woe.

In every cry of every Man,
In every Infant's cry of fear,
In every voice, in every ban,
The mind-forg'd manacles I hear.

How the Chimney-sweeper's cry
Every black'ning Church appalls;
And the hapless Soldier's sigh
Runs in blood down Palace walls.

But most thro' midnight streets I hear
How the youthful Harlot's curse
Blasts the new born Infant's tear,
And blights with plagues the Marriage hearse.

THE MENTAL TRAVELLER

I travel'd thro' a Land of Men,
A Land of Men & Women too,
And heard & saw such dreadful things
As cold Earth wanderers never knew.

For there the Babe is born in joy
That was begotten in dire woe;
Just as we Reap in joy the fruit
Which we in bitter tears did sow.

And if the Babe is born a Boy
He's given to a Woman Old,
Who nails him down upon a rock,
Catches his shrieks in cups of gold.

She binds iron thorns around his head,
She pierces both his hands & feet,
She cuts his heart out at his side
To make it feel both cold & heat.

Her fingers number every Nerve,
Just as a Miser counts his gold;
She lives upon his shrieks & cries,
And she grows young as he grows old.

Till he becomes a bleeding youth,
And she becomes a Virgin bright;
Then he rends up his Manacles
And binds her down for his delight.

He plants himself in all her Nerves,
Just as a Husbandman his mould;

And she becomes his dwelling place
And Garden fruitful seventy fold.

An aged Shadow, soon he fades,
Wand'ring round an Earthly Cot,
Full filled all with gems & gold
Which he by industry had got.

And these are the gems of the Human Soul,
The rubies & pearls of a lovesick eye,
The countless gold of the akeing heart,
The martyr's groan & the lover's sigh.

They are his meat, they are his drink;
He feeds the Beggar & the Poor
And the wayfaring Traveller:
For ever open is his door.

His grief is their eternal joy;
They make the roofs & walls to ring;
Till from the fire on the hearth
A little Female Babe does spring.

And she is all of solid fire
And gems & gold, that none his hand
Dares stretch to touch her Baby form,
Or wrap her in his swaddling-band.

But She comes to the Man she loves,
If young or old, or rich or poor;
They soon drive out the aged Host,
A Beggar at another's door.

He wanders weeping far away,
Untill some other take him in;
Oft blind & age-bent, sore distrest,
Untill he can a Maiden win.

And to allay his freezing Age
The Poor Man takes her in his arms;
The Cottage fades before his sight,
The Garden & its lovely Charms.

The Guests are scatter'd thro' the land,
For the Eye altering alters all;
The Senses roll themselves in fear,
And the flat Earth becomes a Ball;

The stars, sun, Moon, all shrink away,
A desart vast without a bound,
And nothing left to eat or drink,
And a dark desart all around.

The honey of her Infant lips,
The bread & wine of her sweet smile,
The wild game of her roving Eye,
Does him to Infancy beguile;

For as he eats & drinks he grows
Younger & younger every day;
And on the desart wild they both
Wander in terror & dismay.

Like the wild Stag she flees away,
Her fear plants many a thicket wild;
While he pursues her night & day,
By various arts of Love beguil'd,

By various arts of Love & Hate,
Till the wide desart planted o'er
With Labyrinths of wayward Love,
Where roams the Lion, Wolf & Boar,

Till he becomes a wayward Babe,
And she a weeping Woman Old.

Then many a Lover wanders here;
The Sun & Stars are nearer roll'd.

The trees bring forth sweet Extacy
To all who in the desart roam;
Till many a City there is Built,
And many a pleasant Shepherd's home.

But when they find the frowning Babe,
Terror strikes thro' the region wide:
They cry "The Babe! the Babe is Born!"
And flee away on Every side.

For who dare touch the frowning form,
His arm is wither'd to its root;
Lions, Boars, Wolves, all howling flee,
And every Tree does shed its fruit.

And none can touch that frowning form,
Except it be a Woman Old;
She nails him down upon the Rock,
And all is done as I have told.

THE GREY MONK

"I die, I die!" the Mother said,
"My Children die for lack of Bread.
What more has the merciless Tyrant said?"
The Monk sat down on the Stony Bed.

The blood red ran from the Grey Monk's side,
His hands & feet were wounded wide,
His Body bent, his arms & knees
Like to the roots of ancient trees.

His eye was dry; no tear could flow:
A hollow groan first spoke his woe.
He trembled & shudder'd upon the Bed;
At length with a feeble cry he said:

"When God commanded this hand to write
In the studious hours of deep midnight,
He told me the writing I wrote should prove
The Bane of all that on Earth I lov'd.

"My Brother starv'd between two Walls,
His Children's Cry my Soul appalls;
I mock'd at the wrack & griding chain,
My bent body mocks their torturing pain.

"Thy Father drew his sword in the North,
With his thousands strong he marched forth;
Thy Brother has arm'd himself in Steel
To avenge the wrongs thy Children feel.

"But vain the Sword & vain the Bow,
They never can work War's overthrow.
The Hermit's Prayer & the Widow's tear
Alone can free the World from fear.

"For a Tear is an Intellectual Thing,
And a Sigh is the Sword of an Angel King,
And the bitter groan of the Martyr's woe
Is an Arrow from the Almightie's Bow.

"The hand of Vengeance found the Bed
To which the Purple Tyrant fled;
The iron hand crush'd the Tyrant's head
And became a Tyrant in his stead."

Auguries of Innocence

To see a World in a Grain of Sand
And a Heaven in a Wild Flower,
Hold Infinity in the palm of your hand
And Eternity in an hour.

A Robin Red breast in a Cage
Puts all Heaven in a Rage.
A dove house fill'd with doves & Pigeons
Shudders Hell thro' all its regions.
A dog starv'd at his Master's Gate
Predicts the ruin of the State.
A Horse misus'd upon the Road
Calls to Heaven for Human blood.
Each outcry of the hunted Hare
A fibre from the Brain does tear.
A Skylark wounded in the wing,
A Cherubim does cease to sing.
The Game Cock clip'd & arm'd for fight
Does the Rising Sun affright.
Every Wolf's & Lion's howl
Raises from Hell a Human Soul.
The wild deer, wand'ring here & there,
Keeps the Human Soul from Care.
The Lamb misus'd breeds Public strife
And yet forgives the Butcher's Knife.
The Bat that flits at close of Eve
Has left the Brain that won't Believe.
The Owl that calls upon the Night
Speaks the Unbeliever's fright.
He who shall hurt the little Wren
Shall never be belov'd by Men.
He who the Ox to wrath has mov'd

Shall never be by Woman lov'd.
The wanton Boy that kills the Fly
Shall feel the Spider's enmity.
He who torments the Chafer's sprite
Weaves a Bower in endless Night.
The Catterpiller on the Leaf
Repeats to thee thy Mother's grief.
Kill not the Moth nor Butterfly,
For the Last Judgment draweth nigh.
He who shall train the Horse to War
Shall never pass the Polar Bar.
The Beggar's Dog & Widow's Cat,
Feed them & thou wilt grow fat.
The Gnat that sings his Summer's song
Poison gets from Slander's tongue.
The poison of the Snake & Newt
Is the sweat of Envy's Foot.
The Poison of the Honey Bee
Is the Artist's Jealousy.
The Prince's Robes & Beggar's Rags
Are Toadstools on the Miser's Bags.
A truth that's told with bad intent
Beats all the Lies you can invent.
It is right it should be so;
Man was made for Joy & Woe;
And when this we rightly know
Thro' the World we safely go,
Joy & Woe are woven fine,
A Clothing for the Soul divine;
Under every grief & pine
Runs a joy with silken twine.
The Babe is more than swadling Bands;
Throughout all these Human Lands
Tools were made, & Born were hands,
Every Farmer Understands.
Every Tear from Every Eye
Becomes a Babe in Eternity;
This is caught by Females bright

And return'd to its own delight.
The Bleat, the Bark, Bellow & Roar
Are Waves that Beat on Heaven's Shore.
The Babe that weeps the Rod beneath
Writes Revenge in realms of death.
The Beggar's Rags, fluttering in Air,
Does to Rags the Heavens tear.
The Soldier, arm'd with Sword & Gun,
Palsied strikes the Summer's Sun.
The poor Man's Farthing is worth more
Than all the Gold on Afric's Shore.
One Mite wrung from the Labrer's hands
Shall buy & sell the Miser's Lands:
Or, if protected from on high,
Does that whole Nation sell & buy.
He who mocks the Infant's Faith
Shall be mock'd in Age & Death.
He who shall teach the Child to Doubt
The rotting Grave shall ne'er get out.
He who respects the Infant's faith
Triumphs over Hell & Death.
The Child's Toys & the Old Man's Reasons
Are the Fruits of the Two seasons.
The Questioner, who sits so sly,
Shall never know how to Reply.
He who replies to words of Doubt
Doth put the Light of Knowledge out.
The Strongest Poison ever known
Came from Caesar's Laurel Crown.
Nought can deform the Human Race
Like to the Armour's iron brace.
When Gold & Gems adorn the Plow
To peaceful Arts shall Envy Bow.
A Riddle or the Cricket's Cry
Is to Doubt a fit Reply.
The Emmet's Inch & Eagle's Mile
Make Lame Philosophy to smile.
He who Doubts from what he sees

Will ne'er Believe, do what you Please.
If the Sun & Moon should doubt,
They'd immediately Go out.
To be in a Passion you Good may do,
But no Good if a Passion is in you.
The Whore & Gambler, by the State
Licenc'd, build that Nation's Fate.
The Harlot's cry from Street to Street
Shall weave Old England's winding Sheet.
The Winner's Shout, the Loser's Curse,
Dance before dead England's Hearse.
Every Night & every Morn
Some to Misery are Born.
Every Morn & every Night
Some are Born to sweet delight.
Some are Born to sweet delight,
Some are Born to Endless Night.
We are led to Believe a Lie
When we see not Thro' the Eye
Which was Born in a Night to perish in a Night
When the Soul Slept in Beams of Light.
God Appears & God is Light
To those poor Souls who dwell in Night,
But does a Human Form Display
To those who Dwell in Realms of day.

To the Muses

Whether on Ida's shady brow,
   Or in the chambers of the East,
The chambers of the sun, that now
   From antient melody have ceas'd;

Whether in Heav'n ye wander fair,
   Or the green corners of the earth,
Or the blue regions of the air,
   Where the melodious winds have birth;

Whether on chrystal rocks ye rove,
   Beneath the bosom of the sea
Wand'ring in many a coral grove,
   Fair Nine, forsaking Poetry!

How have you left the antient love
   That bards of old enjoy'd in you!
The languid strings do scarcely move!
   The sound is forc'd, the notes are few!

To the Evening Star

Thou fair-hair'd angel of the evening,
Now, whilst the sun rests on the mountains, light
Thy bright torch of love; thy radiant crown
Put on, and smile upon our evening bed!
Smile on our loves, and, while thou drawest the
Blue curtains of the sky, scatter thy silver dew

On every flower that shuts its sweet eyes
In timely sleep. Let thy west wind sleep on
The lake; speak silence with thy glimmering eyes,
And wash the dusk with silver. Soon, full soon,
Dost thou withdraw; then the wolf rages wide,
And the lion glares thro' the dun forest:
The fleeces of our flocks are cover'd with
Thy sacred dew: protect them with thine influence.

from The Four Zoas

*The Torments of Love & Jealousy in the Death and
Judgement of Albion the Ancient Man*

VALA

The Song of the Aged Mother which shook the heavens with
    wrath,
Hearing the march of long resounding, strong heroic Verse
Marshall'd in order for the day of Intellectual Battle.
The heavens quake, the earth was moved & shudder'd, & the
    mountains
With all their woods, the streams & valleys wail'd in dismal
    fear.
Four Mighty Ones are in every Man; a Perfect Unity
Cannot Exist but from the Universal Brotherhood of Eden,
The Universal Man, To Whom be Glory Evermore, Amen.
What are the Natures of those Living Creatures the Heav'nly
    Father only
Knoweth. No Individual knoweth, nor can know in all Eternity.

*

With trembling horror pale, aghast the Children of Man
Stood on the infinite Earth & saw these visions in the air,
In waters & in earth beneath; they cried to one another,
"What! are we terrors to one another? Come, O brethren,
    wherefore
Was this wide Earth spread all abroad? not for wild beasts to
    roam."
But many stood silent, & busied in their families.
And many said, "We see no Visions in the darksom air.

Measure the course of that sulphur orb that lights the darksom
        day;
Set stations on this breeding Earth & let us buy & sell."
Others arose & schools erected, forming Instruments
To measure out the course of heaven. Stern Urizen beheld
In woe his brethren & his sons, in dark'ning woe lamenting
Upon the winds in clouds involv'd, Uttering his voice in
        thunders,
Commanding all the work with care & power & severity.

Then seiz'd the Lions of Urizen their work, & heated in the
        forge
Roar the bright masses; thund'ring beat the hammers, many a
        pyramid
Is form'd & thrown down thund'ring into the deeps of Non
        Entity.
Heated red hot they, hizzing, rend their way down many a
        league
Till resting, each his basement finds; suspended there they
        stand
Casting their sparkles dire abroad into the dismal deep.
For, measur'd out in order'd spaces, the Sons of Urizen
With compasses divide the deep; they the strong scales erect
That Luvah rent from the faint Heart of the Fallen Man,
And weigh the massy Cubes, then fix them in their awful
        stations.

And all the time, in Caverns shut, the golden Looms erected
First spun, then wove the Atmospheres; there the Spider &
        Worm
Plied the wing'd shuttle, piping shrill thro' all the list'ning
        threads;
Beneath the Caverns roll the weights of lead & spindles of iron,
The enormous warp & woof rage direful in the affrighted deep.

While far into the vast unknown the strong wing'd Eagles bend
Their venturous flight in Human forms distinct; thro' darkness
        deep

They bear the woven draperies; on golden hooks they hang
    abroad
The universal curtains & spread out from Sun to Sun
The vehicles of light; they separate the furious particles
Into mild currents as the water mingles with the wine.

While thus the Spirits of strongest wing enlighten the dark
    deep,
The threads are spun & the cords twisted & drawn out; then the
    weak
Begin their work, & many a net is netted, many a net
Spread, & many a Spirit caught: innumerable the nets,
Innumerable the gins & traps, & many a soothing flute
Is form'd, & many a corded lyre outspread over the immense.
In cruel delight they trap the listeners, & in cruel delight
Bind them, condensing the strong energies into little compass.
Some became seed of every plant that shall be planted; some
The bulbous roots, thrown up together into barns & garners.

Then rose the Builders. First the Architect divine his plan
Unfolds. The wondrous scaffold rear'd all round the infinite,
Quadrangular the building rose, the heavens squared by a line,
Trigons & cubes divide the elements in finite bonds.
Multitudes without number work incessant: the hewn stone
Is plac'd in beds of mortar mingled with the ashes of Vala.
Severe the labour; female slaves the mortar trod oppressed.

Twelve halls after the names of his twelve sons compos'd
The wondrous building, & three Central Domes after the
    Names
Of his three daughters were encompass'd by the twelve bright
    halls.
Every hall surrounded by bright Paradises of Delight
In which were towns & Cities, Nations, Seas, Mountains &
    Rivers.
Each Dome open'd toward four halls, & the Three Domes
    Encompass'd
The Golden Hall of Urizen, whose western side glow'd bright

With ever streaming fires beaming from his awful limbs.
His Shadowy Feminine Semblance here repos'd on a White
      Couch,
Or hover'd over his starry head; & when he smil'd she
      brighten'd
Like a bright Cloud in harvest; but when Urizen frown'd she
      wept
In mists over his carved throne; & when he turned his back
Upon his Golden hall & sought the Labyrinthine porches
Of his wide heaven, Trembling, cold, in jealous fears she sat
A shadow of Despair; therefore toward the West, Urizen form'd
A recess in the wall for fires to glow upon the pale
Female's limbs in his absence, & her Daughters oft upon
A Golden Altar burnt perfumes: with Art Celestial form'd
Foursquare, sculptur'd & sweetly Engrav'd to please their
      shadowy mother.
Ascending into her misty garments the blue smoke roll'd to
      revive
Her cold limbs in the absence of her Lord. Also her sons,
With lives of Victims sacrificed upon an altar of brass
On the East side, Reviv'd her soul with lives of beasts & birds
Slain on the Altar, up ascending into her cloudy bosom.
Of terrible workmanship the Altar, labour of ten thousand
      Slaves,
One thousand Men of wondrous power spent their lives in its
      formation.
It stood on twelve steps nam'd after the names of her twelve
      sons,
And was erected at the chief entrance of Urizen's hall.

But infinitely beautiful the wondrous work arose
In sorrow and care, a Golden World whose porches round the
      heavens
And pillar'd halls & rooms reciev'd the eternal wandering stars.
A wondrous golden Building, many a window, many a door
And many a division let in & out the vast unknown.
Circled in infinite orb immoveable, within its walls & cielings

The heavens were clos'd, and spirits mourn'd their bondage
        night & day,
And the Divine Vision appear'd in Luvah's robes of blood.

Thus was the Mundane shell builded by Urizen's strong Power.

                                    *

"I am made to sow the thistle for wheat, the nettle for a
        nourishing dainty.
I have planted a false oath in the earth; it has brought forth a
        poison tree.
I have chosen the serpent for a councellor, & the dog
For a schoolmaster to my children.
I have blotted out from light & living the dove & nightingale,
And I have caused the earth worm to beg from door to door.

"I have taught the thief a secret path into the house of the just.
I have taught pale artifice to spread his nets upon the morning.
My heavens are brass, my earth is iron, my moon a clod of clay,
My sun a pestilence burning at noon & a vapour of death in
        night.

"What is the price of Experience? do men buy it for a song?
Or wisdom for a dance in the street? No, it is bought with the
        price
Of all that a man hath, his house, his wife, his children.
Wisdom is sold in the desolate market where none come to buy,
And in the wither'd field where the farmer plows for bread in
        vain.

"It is an easy thing to triumph in the summer's sun
And in the vintage & to sing on the waggon loaded with corn.
It is an easy thing to talk of patience to the afflicted,
To speak the laws of prudence to the houseless wanderer,
To listen to the hungry raven's cry in wintry season
When the red blood is fill'd with wine & with the marrow of
        lambs.

"It is an easy thing to laugh at wrathful elements,
To hear the dog howl at the wintry door, the ox in the slaughter
     house moan;
To see a god on every wind & a blessing on every blast;
To hear sounds of love in the thunder storm that destroys our
     enemies' house;
To rejoice in the blight that covers his field, & the sickness that
     cuts off his children,
While our olive & vine sing & laugh round our door, & our
     children bring fruits & flowers.

"Then the groan & the dolor are quite forgotten, & the slave
     grinding at the mill,
And the captive in chains, & the poor in the prison, & the
     soldier in the field
When the shatter'd bone hath laid him groaning among the
     happier dead.

"It is an easy thing to rejoice in the tents of prosperity:
Thus could I sing & thus rejoice: but it is not so with me."

                              *

Trembling & strucken by the Universal stroke, the trees unroot,
The rocks groan horrible & run about; the mountains &
Their rivers cry with a dismal cry; the cattle gather together,
Lowing they kneel before the heavens; the wild beasts of the
     forests
Tremble; the Lion shuddering asks the Leopard: "Feelest thou
The dread I feel, unknown before? My voice refuses to roar,
And in weak moans I speak to thee. This night,
Before the morning's dawn, the Eagle call'd the Vulture,
The Raven call'd the hawk, I heard them from my forests black,
Saying: 'Let us go up far, for soon, I smell upon the wind,
A terror coming from the south.' The Eagle & Hawk fled away
At dawn, & e'er the sun arose, the raven & Vulture follow'd.
Let us flee also to the north." They fled. The Sons of Men

Saw them depart in dismal droves. The trumpet sounded loud
And all the Sons of Eternity Descended into Beulah.

In the fierce flames the limbs of Mystery lay consuming with
        howling
And deep despair. Rattling go up the flames around the
        Synagogue
Of Satan. Loud the Serpent Orc rag'd thro' his twenty seven
Folds. The tree of Mystery went up in folding flames.
Blood issu'd out in rushing volumes, pouring in whirlpools
        fierce
From out the flood gates of the Sky. The Gates are burst; down
        pour
The torrents black upon the Earth; the blood pours down
        incessant.
Kings in their palaces lie drown'd. Shepherds, their flocks, their
        tents,
Roll down the mountains in black torrents. Cities, Villages,
High spires & Castles drown'd in the black deluge; shoal on
        shoal
Float the dead carcases of Men & Beasts, driven to & fro on
        waves
Of foaming blood beneath the black incessant sky, till all
Mystery's tyrants are cut off & not one left on Earth.

And when all Tyranny was cut off from the face of the Earth,
Around the dragon form of Urizen, & round his strong form,
The flames rolling intense thro' the wide Universe
Began to enter the Holy City. Ent'ring, the dismal clouds
In furrow'd lightnings break their way, the wild flames licking
        up
The Bloody Deluge: living flames winged with intellect
And Reason, round the Earth they march in order, flame by
        flame.
From the clotted gore & from the hollow den
Start forth the trembling millions into flames of mental fire,
Bathing their limbs in the bright visions of Eternity.

Beyond this Universal Confusion, beyond the remotest Pole
Where their vortexes began to operate, there stands
A Horrible rock far in the South; it was forsaken when
Urizen gave the horses of Light into the hands of Luvah.
On this rock lay the faded head of the Eternal Man
Enwrapped round with weeds of death, pale cold in sorrow &
      woe.
He lifts the blue lamps of his Eyes & cries with heavenly voice:
Bowing his head over the consuming Universe, he cried:
"O weakness & O weariness! O war within my members!
My sons, exiled from my breast, pass to & fro before me.
My birds are silent on my hills, flocks die beneath my branches.
My tents are fallen, my trumpets & the sweet sound of my harp
Is silent on my clouded hills that belch forth storms & fire.
My milk of cows & honey of bees & fruit of golden harvest
Are gather'd in the scorching heat & in the driving rain.
My robe is turned to confusion, & my bright gold to stone.
Where once I sat, I weary walk in misery & pain,
For from within my wither'd breast grown narrow with my
      woes
The Corn is turned to thistles & the apples into poison,
The birds of song to murderous crows, My joys to bitter groans,
The voices of children in my tents to cries of helpless infants,
And all exiled from the face of light & shine of morning
In this dark world, a narrow house, I wander up & down.
I hear Mystery howling in these flames of Consummation.
When shall the Man of future times become as in days of old?
O weary life! why sit I here & give up all my powers
To indolence, to the night of death, when indolence &
      mourning
Sit hovering over my dark threshold? tho' I arise, look out
And scorn the war within my members, yet my heart is weak
And my head faint. Yet will I look again into the morning.
Whence is this sound of rage of Men drinking each other's
      blood.
Drunk with the smoking gore, & red, but not with nourishing
      wine?"

The Eternal Man sat on the Rocks & cried with awful voice:
"O Prince of Light, where art thou? I behold thee not as once
In those Eternal fields, in clouds of morning stepping forth
With harps & songs when bright Ahania sang before thy face
And all thy sons & daughters gather'd round my ample table.
See you not all this wracking furious confusion?
Come forth from slumbers of thy cold abstraction! Come forth,
Arise to Eternal births! Shake off thy cold repose,
Schoolmaster of souls, great opposer of change, arise!
That the Eternal worlds may see thy face in peace & joy,
That thou, dread form of Certainty, maist sit in town & village
While little children play around thy feet in gentle awe,
Fearing thy frown, loving thy smile, O Urizen, Prince of Light."

He call'd; the deep buried his voice & answer none return'd.
Then wrath burst round; the Eternal Man was wrath; again he
        cried:
"Arise, O stony form of death! O dragon of the Deeps!
Lie down before my feet, O Dragon! let Urizen arise.
O how couldst thou deform those beautiful proportions
Of life & person; for as the Person, so is his life proportion'd.
Let Luvah rage in the dark deep, even to Consummation,
For if thou feedest not his rage, it will subside in peace.
But if thou darest obstinate refuse my stern behest,
Thy crown & scepter I will sieze, & regulate all my members
In stern severity, & cast thee out into the indefinite
Where nothing lives, there to wander; & if thou returnest
        weary,
Weeping at the threshold of Existence, I will steel my heart
Against thee to Eternity, & never recieve thee more.
Thy self-destroying, beast form'd Science shall be thy eternal
        lot.
My anger against thee is greater than against this Luvah,
For war is energy Enslav'd, but thy religion,
The first author of this war & the distracting of honest minds
Into confused perturbation & strife & horrour & pride,
Is a deciet so detestable that I will cast thee out

If thou repentest not, & leave thee as a rotten branch to be
    burn'd
With Mystery the Harlot & with Satan for Ever & Ever.
Error can never be redeemed in all Eternity,
But Sin, Even Rahab, is redeem'd in blood & fury & jealousy—
That line of blood that stretch'd across the windows of the
    morning—
Redeem'd from Error's power. Wake, thou dragon of the
    deeps!"

And the Eternal Man said: "Hear my words, O Prince of Light.
Behold Jerusalem in whose bosom the Lamb of God
Is seen; tho' slain before her Gates, he self-renew'd remains
Eternal, & I thro' him awake from death's dark vale.
The times revolve; the time is coming when all these delights
Shall be renew'd, & all these Elements that now consume
Shall reflourish. Then bright Ahania shall awake from death,
A glorious Vision to thine Eyes, a Self-renewing Vision:
The spring, the summer, to be thine; then sleep the wintry days
In silken garments spun by her own hands against her funeral.
The winter thou shalt plow & lay thy stores into thy barns
Expecting to recieve Ahania in the spring with joy.
Immortal thou, Regenerate She, & all the lovely Sex
From her shall learn obedience & prepare for a wintry grave,
That spring may see them rise in tenfold joy & sweet delight
Thus shall the male & female live the life of Eternity,
Because the Lamb of God Creates himself a bride & wife
That we his Children evermore may live in Jerusalem
Which now descendeth out of heaven, a City, yet a Woman,
Mother of myriads redeem'd & born in her spiritual palaces,
By a New Spiritual birth Regenerated from Death."

*

The Sun has left his blackness & has found a fresher morning,
And the mild moon rejoices in the clear & cloudless night,
And Man walks forth from midst of the fires: the evil is all
    consum'd.

His eyes behold the Angelic spheres arising night & day;
The stars consum'd like a lamp blown out, & in their stead,
      behold
The Expanding Eyes of Man behold the depths of wondrous
      worlds!
One Earth, one sea beneath; nor Erring Globes wander, but
      Stars
Of fire rise up nightly from the Ocean; & one Sun
Each morning, like a New born Man, issues with songs & joy
Calling the Plowman to his Labour & the Shepherd to his rest.
He walks upon the Eternal Mountains, raising his heavenly
      voice,
Conversing with the Animal forms of wisdom night & day,
That, risen from the Sea of fire, renew'd walk o'er the Earth;
For Tharmas brought his flocks upon the hills, & in the Vales
Around the Eternal Man's bright tent, the little Children play
Among the wooly flocks. The hammer of Urthona sounds
In the deep caves beneath; his limbs renew'd, his Lions roar
Around the Furnaces & in Evening sport upon the plains.
They raise their faces from the Earth, conversing with the Man:

"How is it we have walk'd thro' fires & yet are not consum'd?
How is it that all things are chang'd, even as in ancient times?"

The Sun arises from his dewy bed, & the fresh airs
Play in his smiling beams giving the seeds of life to grow,
And the fresh Earth beams forth ten thousand thousand springs
      of life.
Urthona is arisen in his strength, no longer now
Divided from Enitharmon, no longer the Spectre Los.
Where is the Spectre of Prophecy? where is the delusive
      Phantom?
Departed: & Urthona rises from the ruinous Walls
In all his ancient strength to form the golden armour of science
For intellectual War. The war of swords departed now,
The dark Religions are departed & sweet Science reigns.

The Marriage of Heaven and Hell

The Argument

Rintrah roars & shakes his fires in the burden'd air;
Hungry clouds swag on the deep.

Once meek, and in a perilous path,
The just man kept his course along
The vale of death.
Roses are planted where thorns grow,
And on the barren heath
Sing the honey bees.

Then the perilous path was planted,
And a river and a spring
On every cliff and tomb,
And on the bleached bones
Red clay brought forth;

Till the villain left the paths of ease,
To walk in perilous paths, and drive
The just man into barren climes.

Now the sneaking serpent walks
In mild humility,
And the just man rages in the wilds
Where lions roam.

Rintrah roars & shakes his fires in the burden'd air;
Hungry clouds swag on the deep.

As a new heaven is begun, and it is now thirty-three years since its advent, the Eternal Hell revives. And lo! Swedenborg is the Angel sitting at the tomb: his writings are the linen clothes folded up. Now is the dominion of Edom, & the return of Adam into Paradise; see Isaiah xxxiv & xxxv Chap.

Without Contraries is no progression. Attraction and Repulsion, Reason and Energy, Love and Hate, are necessary to Human existence.

From these contraries spring what the religious call Good & Evil. Good is the passive that obeys Reason. Evil is the active springing from Energy.

Good is Heaven. Evil is Hell.

The Voice of the Devil

All Bibles or sacred codes have been the causes of the following Errors:

1. That Man has two real existing principles: Viz: a Body & a Soul.

2. That Energy, call'd Evil, is alone from the Body; & that Reason, call'd Good, is alone from the Soul.

3. That God will torment Man in Eternity for following his Energies.

But the following Contraries to these are True:

1. Man has no Body distinct from his Soul; for that call'd Body is a portion of Soul discern'd by the five Senses, the chief inlets of Soul in this age.

2. Energy is the only life, and is from the Body; and Reason is the bound or outward circumference of Energy.

3. Energy is Eternal Delight.

Those who restrain desire, do so because theirs is weak enough to be restrained; and the restrainer or reason usurps its place & governs the unwilling.

And being restrain'd, it by degrees becomes passive, till it is only the shadow of desire.

The history of this is written in Paradise Lost, & the Governor or Reason is call'd Messiah.

And the original Archangel, or possessor of the command of the heavenly host, is call'd the Devil or Satan, and his children are call'd Sin & Death.

But in the Book of Job, Milton's Messiah is call'd Satan.

For this history has been adopted by both parties.

It indeed appear'd to Reason as if Desire was cast out; but the Devil's account is, that the Messiah fell, & formed a heaven of what he stole from the Abyss.

This is shewn in the Gospel, where he prays to the Father to send the comforter, or Desire, that Reason may have Ideas to build on; the Jehovah of the Bible being no other than [the Devil del.] he who dwells in flaming fire.

Know that after Christ's death, he became Jehovah.

But in Milton, the Father is Destiny, the Son a Ratio of the five senses, & the Holy-ghost Vacuum!

Note: The reason Milton wrote in fetters when he wrote of Angels & God, and at liberty when of Devils & Hell, is because he was a true Poet and of the Devil's party without knowing it.

A Memorable Fancy

As I was walking among the fires of hell, delighted with the enjoyments of Genius, which to Angels look like torment and insanity, I collected some of their Proverbs; thinking that as the sayings used in a nation mark its character, so the Proverbs of Hell show the nature of Infernal wisdom better than any description of buildings or garments.

When I came home: on the abyss of the five senses, where a flat sided steep frowns over the present world, I saw a mighty Devil folded in black clouds, hovering on the sides of the rock: with corroding fires he wrote the following sentence now percieved by the minds of men, & read by them on earth:

How do you know but ev'ry Bird that cuts the airy way,
Is an immense world of delight, clos'd by your senses five?

Proverbs of Hell

In seed time learn, in harvest teach, in winter enjoy.
Drive your cart and your plow over the bones of the dead.
The road of excess leads to the palace of wisdom.
Prudence is a rich, ugly old maid courted by Incapacity.
He who desires but acts not, breeds pestilence.
The cut worm forgives the plow.
Dip him in the river who loves water.
A fool sees not the same tree that a wise man sees.
He whose face gives no light, shall never become a star.
Eternity is in love with the productions of time.
The busy bee has no time for sorrow.
The hours of folly are measur'd by the clock; but of wisdom, no
        clock can measure.
All wholesom food is caught without a net or a trap.
Bring out number, weight & measure in a year of dearth.
No bird soars too high, if he soars with his own wings.
A dead body revenges not injuries.
The most sublime act is to set another before you.
If the fool would persist in his folly he would become wise.
Folly is the cloke of knavery.
Shame is Pride's cloke.

Prisons are built with stones of Law, Brothels with bricks of
        Religion.
The pride of the peacock is the glory of God.
The lust of the goat is the bounty of God.
The wrath of the lion is the wisdom of God.
The nakedness of woman is the work of God.
Excess of sorrow laughs. Excess of joy weeps.
The roaring of lions, the howling of wolves, the raging of the
        stormy sea, and the destructive sword, are portions of
        eternity, too great for the eye of man.

The fox condemns the trap, not himself.

Joys impregnate. Sorrows bring forth.

Let man wear the fell of the lion, woman the fleece of the sheep.

The bird a nest, the spider a web, man friendship.

The selfish, smiling fool, & the sullen, frowning fool shall be
    both thought wise, that they may be a rod.

What is now proved was once only imagin'd.

The rat, the mouse, the fox, the rabbet watch the roots; the lion,
    the tyger, the horse, the elephant watch the fruits.

The cistern contains: the fountain overflows.

One thought fills immensity.

Always be ready to speak your mind, and a base man will
    avoid you.

Every thing possible to be believ'd is an image of truth.

The eagle never lost so much time as when he submitted to
    learn of the crow.

The fox provides for himself, but God provides for the lion.

Think in the morning. Act in the noon. Eat in the evening. Sleep
    in the night.

He who has suffer'd you to impose on him, knows you.

As the plow follows words, so God rewards prayers.

The tygers of wrath are wiser than the horses of instruction.

Expect poison from the standing water.

You never know what is enough unless you know what is more
    than enough.

Listen to the fool's reproach! it is a kingly title!

The eyes of fire, the nostrils of air, the mouth of water, the
    beard of earth.

The weak in courage is strong in cunning.

The apple tree never asks the beech how he shall grow; nor the
    lion, the horse, how he shall take his prey.

The thankful reciever bears a plentiful harvest.

If others had not been foolish, we should be so.

The soul of sweet delight can never be defil'd.

When thou seest an Eagle, thou seest a portion of Genius; lift up
    thy head!

As the catterpiller chooses the fairest leaves to lay her eggs on,
    so the priest lays his curse on the fairest joys.
To create a little flower is the labour of ages.
Damn braces: Bless relaxes.
The best wine is the oldest, the best water the newest.
Prayers plow not! Praises reap not!
Joys laugh not! Sorrows weep not!

The head Sublime, the heart Pathos, the genitals Beauty, the
    hands & feet Proportion.
As the air to a bird or the sea to a fish, so is contempt to the
    contemptible.
The crow wish'd every thing was black, the owl that every
    thing was white.
Exuberance is Beauty.
If the lion was advised by the fox, he would be cunning.
Improve[me]nt makes strait roads; but the crooked roads
    without Improvement are roads of Genius.
Sooner murder an infant in its cradle than nurse unacted
    desires.
Where man is not, nature is barren.
Truth can never be told so as to be understood, and not be
    believ'd.
Enough! or Too much.

The ancient Poets animated all sensible objects with Gods or Ge-
niuses, calling them by the names and adorning them with the
properties of woods, rivers, mountains, lakes, cities, nations, and
whatever their enlarged & numerous senses could percieve.
    And particularly they studied the genius of each city & coun-
try, placing it under its mental deity;
    Till a system was formed, which some took advantage of, &
enslav'd the vulgar by attempting to realize or abstract the men-
tal deities from their objects: thus began Priesthood;
    Choosing forms of worship from poetic tales.

And at length they pronounc'd that the Gods had order'd such things.

Thus men forgot that All deities reside in the human breast.

A Memorable Fancy

The Prophets Isaiah and Ezekiel dined with me, and I asked them how they dared so roundly to assert that God spake to them; and whether they did not think at the time that they would be misunderstood, & so be the cause of imposition.

Isaiah answer'd: "I saw no God, nor heard any, in a finite organical "perception; but my senses discover'd the infinite in every thing, and "as I was then perswaded, & remain confirm'd, that the voice of "honest indignation is the voice of God, I cared not for consequences, "but wrote."

Then I asked: "does a firm perswasion that a thing is so, make it so?"

He replied: "All poets believe that it does, & in ages of imagination "this firm perswasion removed mountains; but many are not capable "of a firm perswasion of any thing."

Then Ezekiel said: "The philosophy of the east taught the first "principles of human perception: some nations held one principle "for the origin, & some another: we of Israel taught that the Poetic "Genius (as you now call it) was the first principle and all the others "merely derivative, which was the cause of our despising the Priests "& Philosophers of other countries, and prophecying that all Gods "would at last be proved to originate in ours & to be the tributaries "of the Poetic Genius; it was this that our great poet, King David, "desired so fervently & invokes so pathetic'ly, saying by this he "conquers enemies & governs kingdoms; and we so loved our God, "that we cursed in his name all the deities of surrounding nations, "and asserted that they had rebelled: from these opinions the vulgar "came to think that all nations would at last be subject to the jews."

"This," said he, "like all firm perswasions, is come to pass; for "all nations believe the jews' code and worship the jews' god, and "what greater subjection can be?"

I heard this with some wonder, & must confess my own conviction. After dinner I ask'd Isaiah to favour the world with his lost works; he said none of equal value was lost. Ezekiel said the same of his.

I also asked Isaiah what made him go naked and barefoot three years? he answer'd: "the same that made our friend Diogenes, "the Grecian."

I then asked Ezekiel why he eat dung, & lay so long on his right & left side? he answer'd, "the desire of raising other men into a "perception of the infinite: this the North American tribes practise, "& is he honest who resists his genius or conscience only for the sake "of present ease or gratification?"

The ancient tradition that the world will be consumed in fire at the end of six thousand years is true, as I have heard from Hell.

For the cherub with his flaming sword is hereby commanded to leave his guard at tree of life; and when he does, the whole creation will be consumed and appear infinite and holy, whereas it now appears finite & corrupt.

This will come to pass by an improvement of sensual enjoyment.

But first the notion that man has a body distinct from his soul is to be expunged; this I shall do by printing in the infernal method, by corrosives, which in Hell are salutary and medicinal, melting apparent surfaces away, and displaying the infinite which was hid.

If the doors of perception were cleansed every thing would appear to man as it is, infinite.

For man has closed himself up, till he sees all things thro' narrow chinks of his cavern.

A Memorable Fancy

I was in a Printing house in Hell, & saw the method in which knowledge is transmitted from generation to generation.

In the first chamber was a Dragon-Man, clearing away the rubbish from a cave's mouth; within, a number of Dragons were hollowing the cave.

In the second chamber was a Viper folding round the rock & the cave, and others adorning it with gold, silver and precious stones.

In the third chamber was an Eagle with wings and feathers of air: he caused the inside of the cave to be infinite; around were numbers of Eagle-like men who built palaces in the immense cliffs.

In the fourth chamber were Lions of flaming fire, raging around & melting the metals into living fluids.

In the fifth chamber were Unnam'd forms, which cast the metals into the expanse.

There they were reciev'd by Men who occupied the sixth chamber, and took the forms of books & were arranged in libraries.

The Giants who formed this world into its sensual existence, and now seem to live in it in chains, are in truth the causes of its life & the sources of all activity; but the chains are the cunning of weak and tame minds which have power to resist energy; according to the proverb, the weak in courage is strong in cunning.

Thus one portion of being is the Prolific, the other the Devouring: to the devourer it seems as if the producer was in his chains; but it is not so, he only takes portions of existence and fancies that the whole.

But the Prolific would cease to be Prolific unless the Devourer, as a sea, reciev'd the excess of his delights.

Some will say: "Is not God alone the Prolific?" I answer: "God "only Acts & Is, in existing beings or Men."

These two classes of men are always upon earth, & they should be enemies: whoever tries to reconcile them seeks to destroy existence.

Religion is an endeavour to reconcile the two.

Note: Jesus Christ did not wish to unite, but to seperate them, as in the Parable of sheep and goats! & he says: "I came not to send Peace, but a Sword."

Messiah or Satan or Tempter was formerly thought to be one of the Antediluvians who are our Energies.

A Memorable Fancy

An Angel came to me and said: "O pitiable foolish young man! O "horrible! O dreadful state! consider the hot burning dungeon thou "art preparing for thyself to all eternity, to which thou art going in "such career."

I said: "perhaps you will be willing to shew me my eternal lot, & "we will contemplate together upon it, and see whether your lot or "mine is most desirable."

So he took me thro' a stable & thro' a church & down into the church vault, at the end of which was a mill: thro' the mill we went, and came to a cave: down the winding cavern we groped our tedious way, till a void boundless as a nether sky appear'd beneath us, & we held by the roots of trees and hung over this immensity; but I said: "if you please, we will commit ourselves to this void, and see "whether providence is here also: if you will not, I will:" but he answer'd: "do not presume, O young man, but as we here remain, "behold thy lot which will soon appear when the darkness passes "away."

So I remain'd with him, sitting in the twisted root of an oak; he was suspended in a fungus, which hung with the head downward into the deep.

By degrees we beheld the infinite Abyss, fiery as the smoke of a burning city; beneath us, at an immense distance, was the sun, black but shining; round it were fiery tracks on which revolv'd vast spiders, crawling after their prey, which flew, or rather swum, in the infinite deep, in the most terrific shapes of animals sprung from corruption; & the air was full of them, & seem'd composed of them: these are Devils, and are called Powers of the air. I now asked my companion which was my eternal lot? he said: "between the black & white spiders."

But now, from between the black & white spiders, a cloud and fire burst and rolled thro' the deep, black'ning all beneath, so that the nether deep grew black as a sea, & rolled with a terrible noise; beneath us was nothing now to be seen but a black tempest, till looking east between the clouds & the waves, we saw a cataract of blood mixed with fire, and not many stones' throw from us appear'd and sunk again the scaly fold of a monstrous serpent; at last, to the east, distant about three degrees, appear'd a fiery crest above the waves; slowly it reared like a ridge of golden rocks, till we discover'd two globes of crimson fire, from which the sea fled away in clouds of smoke; and now we saw it was the head of Leviathan; his forehead was divided into streaks of green & purple like those on a tyger's forehead: soon we saw his mouth & red gills hang just above the raging foam, tinging the black deep with beams of blood, advancing toward us with all the fury of a spiritual existence.

My friend the Angel climb'd up from his station into the mill: I remain'd alone; & then this appearance was no more, but I found myself sitting on a pleasant bank beside a river by moonlight, hearing a harper, who sung to the harp; & his theme was: "The man who "never alters his opinion is like standing water, & breeds reptiles of "the mind."

But I arose and sought for the mill, & there I found my Angel, who, surprised, asked me how I escaped?

I answer'd: "All that we saw was owing to your metaphysics; for "when you ran away, I found myself on a bank by moonlight hearing "a harper. But now we have seen my eternal lot, shall I shew you "yours?" he laugh'd at my proposal; but I by force suddenly caught him in my arms, & flew westerly thro' the night, till we were elevated above the earth's shadow; then I flung myself with him directly into the body of the sun; here I clothed myself in white, & taking in my hand Swedenborg's volumes, sunk from the glorious clime, and passed all the planets till we came to saturn: here I stay'd to rest, & then leap'd into the void between saturn & the fixed stars.

"Here," said I, "is your lot, in this space—if space it may be "call'd." Soon we saw the stable and the church, & I took him to the altar and open'd the Bible, and lo! it was a deep pit, into which I descended, driving the Angel before me; soon we saw seven houses of brick; one we enter'd; in it were a number of monkeys, baboons, & all of that species, chain'd by the middle, grinning and snatching at one another, but witheld by the shortness of their chains: however, I saw that they sometimes grew numerous, and then the weak were caught by the strong, and with a grinning aspect, first coupled with, & then devour'd, by plucking off first one limb and then another, till the body was left a helpless trunk; this, after grinning & kissing it with seeming fondness, they devour'd too; and here & there I saw one savourily picking the flesh off of his own tail; as the stench terribly annoy'd us both, we went into the mill, & I in my hand brought the skeleton of a body, which in the mill was Aristotle's Analytics.

So the Angel said: "thy phantasy has imposed upon me, & thou "oughtest to be ashamed."

I answer'd: "we impose on one another, & it is but lost time to "converse with you whose works are only Analytics."

Opposition is True Friendship

I have always found that Angels have the vanity to speak of themselves as the only wise; this they do with a confident insolence sprouting from systematic reasoning.

Thus Swedenborg boasts that what he writes is new; tho' it is only the Contents or Index of already publish'd books.

A man carried a monkey about for a shew, & because he was a little wiser than the monkey, grew vain, and conciev'd himself as much wiser than seven men. It is so with Swedenborg: he shews the folly of churches, & exposes hypocrites, till he imagines that all are religious, & himself the single one on earth that ever broke a net.

Now hear a plain fact: Swedenborg has not written one new truth. Now hear another: he has written all the old falshoods.

And now hear the reason. He conversed with Angels who are all religious, & conversed not with Devils who all hate religion, for he was incapable thro' his conceited notions.

Thus Swedenborg's writings are a recapitulation of all superficial opinions, and an analysis of the more sublime—but no further.

Have now another plain fact. Any man of mechanical talents

may, from the writings of Paracelsus or Jacob Behmen, produce ten thousand volumes of equal value with Swedenborg's, and from those of Dante or Shakespear an infinite number.

But when he has done this, let him not say that he knows better than his master, for he only holds a candle in sunshine.

A Memorable Fancy

Once I saw a Devil in a flame of fire, who arose before an Angel that sat on a cloud, and the Devil utter'd these words: "The worship of God is: Honouring his gifts in other men, each according to his "genius, and loving the greatest men best: those who envy or "calumniate great men hate God; for there is no other God."

The Angel hearing this became almost blue; but mastering himself he grew yellow, & at last white, pink, & smiling, and then replied:

"Thou Idolater! is not God One? & is not he visible in Jesus "Christ? and has not Jesus Christ given his sanction to the law of "ten commandments? and are not all other men fools, sinners, & "nothings?"

The Devil answer'd: "bray a fool in a morter with wheat, yet shall "not his folly be beaten out of him; if Jesus Christ is the greatest "man, you ought to love him in the greatest degree; now hear how "he has given his sanction to the law of ten commandments: did he "not mock at the sabbath, and so mock the sabbath's God? murder "those who were murder'd because of him? turn away the law from "the woman taken in adultery? steal the labor of others to support "him? bear false witness when he omitted making a defence before "Pilate? covet when he pray'd for his disciples, and when he bid "them shake off the dust of their feet against such as refused to lodge "them? I tell you, no virtue can exist without breaking these ten "commandments. Jesus was all virtue, and acted from impulse, not "from rules."

When he had so spoken, I beheld the Angel, who stretched out his arms, embracing the flame of fire, & he was consumed and arose as Elijah.

Note: This Angel, who is now become a Devil, is my particular friend; we often read the Bible together in its infernal or diaboli-cal sense, which the world shall have if they behave well.

I have also The Bible of Hell, which the world shall have whether they will or no.

One Law for the Lion & Ox is Oppression.

A Song of Liberty

I

1. The Eternal Female groan'd! it was heard over all the Earth.

2. Albion's coast is sick silent; the American meadows faint!

3. Shadows of Prophecy shiver along by the lakes and the rivers and mutter across the ocean: France, rend down thy dungeon!

4. Golden Spain, burst the barriers of old Rome!

5. Cast thy keys, O Rome, into the deep down falling, even to eternity down falling.

6. And weep and bow thy reverend locks.

7. In her trembling hands she took the new born terror, howling:

8. On those infinite mountains of light, now barr'd out by the atlantic sea, the new born fire stood before the starry king!

9. Flag'd with grey brow'd snows and thunderous visages, the jealous wings wav'd over the deep.

10. The speary hand burned aloft, unbuckled was the shield; forth went the hand of jealousy among the flaming hair, and hurl'd the new born wonder thro' the starry night.

11. The fire, the fire is falling!

12. Look up! look up! O citizen of London, enlarge thy countenance! O Jew, leave counting gold! return to thy oil and wine. O African! black African! (go, winged thought, widen his forehead.)

13. The fiery limbs, the flaming hair, shot like the sinking sun into the western sea.

14. Wak'd from his eternal sleep, the hoary element roaring fled away:

15. Down rush'd, beating his wings in vain, the jealous king; his grey brow'd councellors, thunderous warriors, curl'd veterans, among helms, and shields, and chariots, horses, elephants, banners, castles, slings, and rocks,

16. Falling, rushing, ruining! buried in the ruins, on Urthona's dens;

17. All night beneath the ruins; then, their sullen flames faded, emerge round the gloomy King.

18. With thunder and fire, leading his starry hosts thro' the waste wilderness, he promulgates his ten commands, glancing his beamy eyelids over the deep in dark dismay,

19. Where the son of fire in his eastern cloud, while the morning plumes her golden breast,

20. Spurning the clouds written with curses, stamps the stony law to dust, loosing the eternal horses from the dens of night, crying:

EMPIRE IS NO MORE! AND NOW THE LION & WOLF SHALL CEASE.

Chorus

Let the Priests of the Raven of dawn, no longer in deadly black, with hoarse note curse the sons of joy. Nor his accepted brethren—whom, tyrant, he calls free—lay the bound or build the roof. Nor pale religious letchery call that virginity that wishes but acts not!

For every thing that lives is Holy.

VISIONS OF THE DAUGHTERS
OF ALBION

The Eye sees more than the Heart Knows

The Argument

I loved Theotormon,
And I was not ashamed;
I trembled in my virgin fears,
And I hid in Leutha's vale!

I plucked Leutha's flower,
And I rose up from the vale;
But the terrible thunders tore
My virgin mantle in twain.

Visions

Enslav'd, the Daughters of Albion weep; a trembling
     lamentation
Upon their mountains; in their valleys, sighs toward America.

For the soft soul of America, Oothoon, wander'd in woe,
Along the vales of Leutha seeking flowers to comfort her;
And thus she spoke to the bright Marygold of Leutha's vale:

"Art thou a flower? art thou a nymph? I see thee now a flower,
"Now a nymph! I dare not pluck thee from thy dewy bed!"

The Golden nymph replied: "Pluck thou my flower, Oothoon
     the mild!
"Another flower shall spring, because the soul of sweet delight

"Can never pass away." She ceas'd, & clos'd her golden shrine.
Then Oothoon pluck'd the flower, saying: "I pluck thee from
      thy bed,
"Sweet flower, and put thee here to glow between my breasts,
"And thus I turn my face to where my whole soul seeks."

Over the waves she went in wing'd exulting swift delight,
And over Theotormon's reign took her impetuous course.

   Bromion rent her with his thunders; on his stormy bed
Lay the faint maid, and soon her woes appall'd his thunders
      hoarse.

Bromion spoke: "Behold this harlot here on Bromion's bed,
"And let the jealous dolphins sport around the lovely maid!
"Thy soft American plains are mine, and mine thy north &
      south:
"Stampt with my signet are the swarthy children of the sun;
"They are obedient, they resist not, they obey the scourge;
"Their daughters worship terrors and obey the violent.
"Now thou maist marry Bromion's harlot, and protect the child
"Of Bromion's rage, that Oothoon shall put forth in nine
      moons' time."

Then storms rent Theotormon's limbs: he roll'd his waves
      around
And folded his black jealous waters round the adulterate pair.
Bound back to back in Bromion's caves, terror & meekness
      dwell:

At entrance Theotormon sits, wearing the threshold hard
With secret tears; beneath him sound like waves on a desart
      shore
The voice of slaves beneath the sun, and children bought with
      money,

That shiver in religious caves beneath the burning fires
Of lust, that belch incessant from the summits of the earth.

Oothoon weeps not; she cannot weep! her tears are locked up;
But she can howl incessant writhing her soft snowy limbs,
And calling Theotormon's Eagles to prey upon her flesh.

"I call with holy voice! Kings of the sounding air,
"Rend away this defiled bosom that I may reflect
"The image of Theotormon on my pure transparent breast."

The Eagles at her call descend & rend their bleeding prey:
Theotormon severely smiles; her soul reflects the smile,
As the clear spring, mudded with feet of beasts, grows pure &
        smiles.

The Daughters of Albion hear her woes, & eccho back her sighs.

"Why does my Theotormon sit weeping upon the threshold,
"And Oothoon hovers by his side, perswading him in vain?
"I cry: arise, O Theotormon! for the village dog
"Barks at the breaking day; the nightingale has done lamenting;
"The lark does rustle in the ripe corn, and the Eagle returns
"From nightly prey and lifts his golden beak to the pure east,
"Shaking the dust from his immortal pinions to awake
"The sun that sleeps too long. Arise, my Theotormon, I am
        pure,
"Because the night is gone that clos'd me in its deadly black.
"They told me that the night & day were all that I could see;
"They told me that I had five senses to inclose me up,
"And they inclos'd my infinite brain into a narrow circle,
"And sunk my heart into the Abyss, a red, round globe, hot
        burning,
"Till all from life I was obliterated and erased.
"Instead of morn arises a bright shadow, like an eye
"In the eastern cloud; instead of night a sickly charnel house:
"That Theotormon hears me not! to him the night and morn
"Are both alike; a night of sighs, a morning of fresh tears,
"And none but Bromion can hear my lamentations.

"With what sense is it that the chicken shuns the ravenous
    hawk?
"With what sense does the tame pigeon measure out the
    expanse?
"With what sense does the bee form cells? have not the mouse
    & frog
"Eyes and ears and sense of touch? yet are their habitations
"And their pursuits as different as their forms and as their joys.
"Ask the wild ass why he refuses burdens, and the meek camel
"Why he loves man: is it because of eye, ear, mouth, or skin,
"Or breathing nostrils? No, for these the wolf and tyger have.
"Ask the blind worm the secrets of the grave, and why her
    spires
"Love to curl round the bones of death; and ask the rav'nous
    snake
"Where she gets poison, & the wing'd eagle why he loves the
    sun;
"And then tell me the thoughts of man, that have been hid of
    old.

"Silent I hover all the night, and all day could be silent
"If Theotormon once would turn his loved eyes upon me.
"How can I be defil'd when I reflect thy image pure?
"Sweetest the fruit that the worm feeds on, & the soul prey'd on
    by woe,
"The new wash'd lamb ting'd with the village smoke, & the
    bright swan
"By the red earth of our immortal river. I bathe my wings,
"And I am white and pure to hover round Theotormon's
    breast."

Then Theotormon broke his silence, and he answered:—

"Tell me what is the night or day to one o'erflow'd with woe?
"Tell me what is a thought, & of what substance is it made?
"Tell me what is a joy, & in what gardens do joys grow?
"And in what rivers swim the sorrows? and upon what
    mountains

"Wave shadows of discontent? and in what houses dwell the
        wretched,
"Drunken with woe forgotten, and shut up from cold despair?

"Tell me where dwell the thoughts forgotten till thou call them
        forth?
"Tell me where dwell the joys of old? & where the ancient
        loves,
"And when will they renew again, & the night of oblivion past,
"That I might traverse times & spaces far remote, and bring
"Comforts into a present sorrow and a night of pain?
"Where goest thou, O thought? to what remote land is thy
        flight?
"If thou returnest to the present moment of affliction
"Wilt thou bring comforts on thy wings, and dews and honey
        and balm,
"Or poison from the desart wilds, from the eyes of the envier?"

Then Bromion said, and shook the cavern with his lamentation:

"Thou knowest that the ancient trees seen by thine eyes have
        fruit,
"But knowest thou that trees and fruits flourish upon the earth
"To gratify senses unknown? trees, beasts and birds unknown;
"Unknown, not unperciev'd, spread in the infinite microscope,
"In places yet unvisited by the voyager, and in worlds
"Over another kind of seas, and in atmospheres unknown:
"Ah! are there other wars beside the wars of sword and fire?
"And are there other sorrows beside the sorrows of poverty?
"And are there other joys beside the joys of riches and ease?
"And is there not one law for both the lion and the ox?
"And is there not eternal fire and eternal chains
"To bind the phantoms of existence from eternal life?"

Then Oothoon waited silent all the day and all the night;
But when the morn arose, her lamentation renew'd.
The Daughters of Albion hear her woes, & eccho back her sighs.

144   *William Blake*

"O Urizen! Creator of men! mistaken Demon of heaven!
"Thy joys are tears, thy labour vain to form men to thine image.
"How can one joy absorb another? are not different joys
"Holy, eternal, infinite? and each joy is a Love.

"Does not the great mouth laugh at a gift, & the narrow eyelids
        mock
"At the labour that is above payment? and wilt thou take the
        ape
"For thy councellor, or the dog for a schoolmaster to thy
        children?
"Does he who contemns poverty and he who turns with
        abhorrence
"From usury feel the same passion, or are they moved alike?
"How can the giver of gifts experience the delights of the
        merchant?
"How the industrious citizen the pains of the husbandman?
"How different far the fat fed hireling with hollow drum,
"Who buys whole corn fields into wastes, and sings upon the
        heath!
"How different their eye and ear! how different the world to
        them!
"With what sense does the parson claim the labour of the
        farmer?
"What are his nets & gins & traps; & how does he surround
        him
"With cold floods of abstraction, and with forests of solitude,
"To build him castles and high spires, where kings & priests
        may dwell;
"Till she who burns with youth, and knows no fixed lot, is
        bound
"In spells of law to one she loathes? and must she drag the
        chain
"Of life in weary lust? must chilling, murderous thoughts
        obscure
"The clear heaven of her eternal spring; to bear the wintry rage
"Of a harsh terror, driv'n to madness, bound to hold a rod
"Over her shrinking shoulders all the day, & all the night

"To turn the wheel of false desire, and longings that wake her
  womb
"To the abhorred birth of cherubs in the human form,
"That live a pestilence & die a meteor, & are no more;
"Till the child dwell with one he hates, and do the deed he
  loaths,
"And the impure scourge force his seed into its unripe birth
"Ere yet his eyelids can behold the arrows of the day?

"Does the whale worship at thy footsteps as the hungry dog;
"Or does he scent the mountain prey because his nostrils wide
"Draw in the ocean? does his eye discern the flying cloud
"As the raven's eye? or does he measure the expanse like the
  vulture?
"Does the still spider view the cliffs where eagles hide their
  young;
"Or does the fly rejoice because the harvest is brought in?
"Does not the eagle scorn the earth & despise the treasures
  beneath?
"But the mole knoweth what is there, & the worm shall tell it
  thee.
"Does not the worm erect a pillar in the mouldering church
  yard
"And a palace of eternity in the jaws of the hungry grave?
"Over his porch these words are written: 'Take thy bliss, O
  Man!
" 'And sweet shall be thy taste, & sweet thy infant joys renew!'

"Infancy! fearless, lustful, happy, nestling for delight
"In laps of pleasure: Innocence! honest, open, seeking
"The vigorous joys of morning light; open to virgin bliss.
"Who taught thee modesty, subtil modesty, child of night &
  sleep?
"When thou awakest wilt thou dissemble all thy secret joys,
"Or wert thou not awake when all this mystery was disclos'd?
"Then com'st thou forth a modest virgin, knowing to
  dissemble,
"With nets found under thy night pillow, to catch virgin joy
"And brand it with the name of whore, & sell it in the night,

"In silence, ev'n without a whisper, and in seeming sleep.
"Religious dreams and holy vespers light thy smoky fires:
"Once were thy fires lighted by the eyes of honest morn.
"And does my Theotormon seek this hypocrite modesty,
"This knowing, artful, secret, fearful, cautious, trembling
        hypocrite?
"Then is Oothoon a whore indeed! and all the virgin joys
"Of life are harlots, and Theotormon is a sick man's dream;
"And Oothoon is the crafty slave of selfish holiness.

"But Oothoon is not so: a virgin fill'd with virgin fancies,
"Open to joy and to delight where ever beauty appears;
"If in the morning sun I find it, there my eyes are fix'd
"In happy copulation; if in evening mild, wearied with work,
"Sit on a bank and draw the pleasures of this free born joy.

"The moment of desire! the moment of desire! The virgin
"That pines for man shall awaken her womb to enormous joys
"In the secret shadows of her chamber: the youth shut up from
"The lustful joy shall forget to generate & create an amorous
        image
"In the shadows of his curtains and in the folds of his silent
        pillow.
"Are not these the places of religion, the rewards of continence,
"The self enjoyings of self denial? why dost thou seek religion?
"Is it because acts are not lovely that thou seekest solitude
"Where the horrible darkness is impressed with reflections of
        desire?

"Father of Jealousy, be thou accursed from the earth!
"Why hast thou taught my Theotormon this accursed thing?
"Till beauty fades from off my shoulders, darken'd and cast
        out,
"A solitary shadow wailing on the margin of non-entity.

"I cry: Love! Love! Love! happy happy Love! free as the
        mountain wind!
"Can that be Love that drinks another as a sponge drinks water,
"That clouds with jealousy his nights, with weepings all the
        day,

"To spin a web of age around him, grey and hoary, dark,
"Till his eyes sicken at the fruit that hangs before his sight?
"Such is self-love that envies all, a creeping skeleton
"With lamplike eyes watching around the frozen marriage bed.

"But silken nets and traps of adamant will Oothoon spread,
"And catch for thee girls of mild silver, or of furious gold.
"I'll lie beside thee on a bank & view their wanton play
"In lovely copulation, bliss on bliss, with Theotormon:
"Red as the rosy morning, lustful as the first born beam,
"Oothoon shall view his dear delight, nor e'er with jealous
            cloud
"Come in the heaven of generous love, nor selfish blightings
            bring.

"Does the sun walk in glorious raiment on the secret floor
"Where the cold miser spreads his gold; or does the bright
            cloud drop
"On his stone threshold? does his eye behold the beam that
            brings
"Expansion to the eye of pity? or will he bind himself
"Beside the ox to thy hard furrow? does not that mild beam blot
"The bat, the owl, the glowing tyger, and the king of night?
"The sea fowl takes the wintry blast for a cov'ring to her limbs,
"And the wild snake the pestilence to adorn him with gems &
            gold;
"And trees & birds & beasts & men behold their eternal joy.
"Arise, you little glancing wings, and sing your infant joy!
"Arise, and drink your bliss, for every thing that lives is holy!"

Thus every morning wails Oothoon; but Theotormon sits
Upon the margin'd ocean conversing with shadows dire.

The Daughters of Albion hear her woes, & eccho back her sighs.

THE END

ARTHUR RIMBAUD

———————————

I had caught a glimpse of conversion to good
and to happiness, salvation. Can I describe the
vision? The air of Hell will tolerate no hymns!
There were a million charming creatures, a
melodious sacred concert, strength and peace,
noble ambitions—I don't know what all!

"NIGHT OF HELL"

Arthur Rimbaud

(France, 1854–1891)

Arthur Rimbaud was born in Charleville, a small French town near the border of Belgium. He is perhaps as famous for quitting poetry before turning twenty as for his important body of Symbolist—and visionary—poetry.

As a boy he was a precocious student. He was also a rebel, often running away from home and wandering for days without a place to stay. He published his first poem at age fifteen and the next year, at the urging of a friend, wrote to Paul Verlaine, who invited him to Paris. Verlaine introduced the young poet to a number of literary figures, most of whom were put off by his arrogance and the debauchery he cultivated. Rimbaud and Verlaine became intimate friends, much to the dismay of Verlaine's family and friends. After a number of misadventures, the two departed Paris and settled in London. During this period Rimbaud was working on both *Illuminations* and *A Season in Hell.* When Rimbaud decided it was necessary to terminate the relationship, Verlaine shot Rimbaud in the wrist and ended up in prison. Soon after, Rimbaud completed *A Season in Hell*, a kind of spiritual autobiography, which he had printed in Belgium in 1873 and distributed to the Parisian literary world. The book was not received well—probably more a reaction to Rimbaud's personality than to his poems. It is difficult to identify the correct sequence and publication date of the poems of *Illuminations*, which were kept by a number of friends and submitted to magazines with few notations about their chronology. In any case Rimbaud, in despair over his relationship with Verlaine or the poor response to his book or some combination of the two, returned home to Charleville, where he burned his manuscripts and all remaining copies of his book. As far as is known, he never again wrote a poem.

Rimbaud became a wanderer, traveling to Germany and Italy, crossing the Alps on foot. On his way to Russia he was robbed in Vienna and forced to return to France. He then joined the Dutch army, which he soon deserted and again returned to France. During the next years he worked for a circus, as a laborer in Alexandria, in a desert quarry on Cyprus, at a trading post in Abyssinia, and as a gunrunner. By now his reputation as a brilliant poet, whose work encompassed the extremes of existence with an exquisite lexicon and much formal originality, had grown, but he resisted entreaties to return to the literary world. At the age of thirty-seven he died in a hospital in Marseilles.

When Rimbaud was sixteen he articulated his ambition as a poet by turning himself into a *voyant*—a poet/seer/visionary, a poet whose task it is to take on the "unknown." In a letter to a teacher he wrote, "I want to be a poet, and I am working to make myself a *visionary* . . . to arrive at the unknown . . . through a long, a prodigious and rational disordering of *all* the senses."

A Season in Hell

Once, if I remember well, my life was a feast where all hearts opened and all wines flowed.

One evening I seated Beauty on my knees. And I found her bitter. And I cursed her.

I armed myself against justice.

I fled. O Witches, O Misery, O Hate, to you has my treasure been entrusted!

I contrived to purge my mind of all human hope. On all joy, to strangle it, I pounced with the stealth of a wild beast.

I called to the executioners that I might gnaw their rifle-butts while dying. I called to the plagues to smother me in blood, in sand. Misfortune was my God. I laid myself down in the mud. I dried myself in the air of crime. I played sly tricks on madness.

And spring brought me the idiot's frightful laughter.

Now, only recently, being on the point of giving my last squawk, I thought of looking for the key to the ancient feast where I might find my appetite again.

Charity is that key.—This inspiration proves that I have dreamed!

"You will always be a hyena . . ." etc., protests the devil who crowned me with such pleasant poppies. "Attain death with all your appetites, your selfishness and all the capital sins!"

Ah! I'm fed up:—But, dear Satan, a less fiery eye I beg you! And while awaiting a few small infamies in arrears, you who love the absence of the instructive or descriptive faculty in a writer, for you let me tear out these few, hideous pages from my notebook of one of the damned.

NIGHT OF HELL

I have swallowed a monstrous dose of poison.—Thrice blessed be the counsel that came to me!—My entrails are on fire. The violence of the venom twists my limbs, deforms and prostrates me. I die of thirst, I suffocate, and cannot scream. It is hell, eternal punishment! See how the fire flares up again! How nicely I burn. Go to it, demon!

I had caught a glimpse of conversion to good and to happiness, salvation. Can I describe the vision? The air of Hell will tolerate no hymns! There were a million charming creatures, a melodious sacred concert, strength and peace, noble ambitions—I don't know what all!

Noble ambitions!

And still this is life!—Suppose damnation were eternal! Then a man who would mutilate himself is well damned, isn't he? I think I am in hell, therefore I am in hell. It is the execution of the catechism. I am the slave of my baptism. Parents, you have been my undoing and your own. Poor innocent!—Hell has no power over pagans.

—This is life still! Later the delights of damnation will be more profound. A crime, quick, a crime, that I may fall into nothingness in accordance with human law.

Be quiet, do be quiet! . . . There's shame and reprobation here: Satan who says that the fire is contemptible, that my anger is horribly silly. Enough! . . . Fallacies they whisper to me, sorceries, false perfumes, childish music.—And to think that I possess truth, that I perceive justice: my judgment is sound and sure, I am ripe for perfection . . . Pride.—My scalp is drying up. Pity! Lord, I am afraid. I am thirsty, so thirsty! Ah, childhood, the grass, the rain, the lake over the stones, *the moonlight when the bell was chiming twelve* . . . the devil is in the belfry at this hour. Mary! Holy Virgin! . . . —Horror of my stupidity.

Out there, are they not honest souls that wish me well? . . .

Come . . . I have a pillow over my mouth, they do not hear me, they are phantoms. Besides, no one ever thinks of others. Let no one come near me. I must smell scorched I'm sure.

Hallucinations are without number. Truly that is what I have always known: no more faith in history, principles forgotten. I'll keep quiet about that: poets and visionaries would be jealous. I am a thousand times the richest, let us be as avaricious as the sea.

What! The clock of life stopped a while ago. I am no longer in the world.—Theology is serious, hell is certainly *down below*,— and heaven on high.—Ecstasy, nightmare, and sleep in a nest of flames.

What tricks of observation in the country . . . Satan, Old Nick, runs with the wild grain . . . Jesus walks on the purple briars and they do not bend . . . Jesus walked on the troubled waters. The lantern showed him to us, erect, white, with long brown hair, on the flank of an emerald wave. . . .

I am going to unveil all the mysteries: religious mysteries, or natural mysteries, death, birth, the future, the past, cosmogony, nothingness. I am a master of phantasmagoria.

Listen! . . .

I have all the talents!—There is no one here and there is some-one: I would not squander my treasures.—Do you want negro songs, the dances of houris? Do you want me to vanish, to dive after the *ring*? Is that what you want? I will make gold, remedies.

Have faith in me then, faith assuages, guides, restores. Come, all of you—even the little children—that I may comfort you, that my heart may be poured out for you,—the marvelous heart!— Poor men, toilers! I do not ask for prayers; with your trust alone I shall be happy.

—And what of me? All this hardly makes me regret the world very much. I am lucky not to suffer more. My life was nothing but sweet follies, it's a pity.

Bah! Let's practice every imaginable grimace.

Decidedly we are out of the world. No longer any sound. My sense of touch has left me. Ah! my castle, my Saxony, my willow wood. Evenings, mornings, nights, days . . . How weary I am!

I should have my hell for anger, my hell for pride,—and the hell of laziness; a symphony of hells.

I die of lassitude. It is the tomb, I go to the worms, horror of horrors! Satan, you fraud, you would dissolve me with your charms. I insist. I insist! a thrust of the pitchfork, a drop of fire.

Ah! to rise again into life! to cast our eyes on our deformities. And that poison, that kiss, a thousand times accursed! My weakness, the cruelty of the world! My God, pity, hide me, I behave too badly!—I am hidden and I am not.

It is the fire that flares up again with its damned.

from DELIRIUM

HUNGER

If I've a taste, it's not alone
For the earth and stones,
Rocks, coal, iron, air,
That's my daily fare.

Turn my hungers, hungers browse
On the field of sound,
Suck up bindweed's gay venom
Along the ground.

Eat the pebbles that one breaks,
Churches' old stones;
Gravel of ancient deluge taste,
And loaves scattered in grey brakes.

*

Howling underneath the leaves
The wolf spits out the lovely plumes
Of his feast of fowls:
Like him I am consumed.

Salads and fruits
Await but the picking;
But violets are the food
Of spiders in the thicket.

Let me sleep! Let me seethe
At the altars of Solomon.
Broth run over the rust
And mix with the Cedron.

At last, O happiness, O reason, I brushed from the sky the
azure that is darkness, and I lived—gold spark of *pure* light.
Out of joy I took on an expression as clownish and blank as
possible:

*

It is recovered!
What? Eternity.
It is the sea
Mixed with the sun.

My soul eternal,
Redeem your promise,
In spite of the night alone
And the day on fire.

Of human suffrage,
Of common aspirings,
You free yourself then!
You fly according to . . .

Hope never more,
No *orietur*.
Science and patience,
Retribution is sure.

No more tomorrows,
Embers of satin,
Your ardor is now
Your duty only.

It is recovered!
What? Eternity.
It is the sea
Mixed with the sun.

I became a fabulous opera; I saw that all creatures have a fatality of happiness: action is not life, but only a way of spoiling some force, an enervation. Morality is the weakness of the brain.

It seemed to me that to every creature several *other* lives were due. This gentleman knows not what he does: he is an angel. This family is a litter of puppies. With several men I have spoken aloud with a moment of one of their other lives. Thus it was I loved a pig.

Not a single sophistry of madness—madness to be confined— was forgotten: I could recite them all again, I know the system.

My health was threatened. Terror came. I would fall into a slumber of days, and getting up would go on with the same sad dreams. I was ripe for death and along a road of perils my weakness led me to the confines of the world and of Cimmeria, home of whirlwinds and of darkness.

I had to travel, divert the spells assembled in my brain. Over the sea, that I loved as though it were to cleanse me of a stain, I saw the comforting cross arise. I had been damned by the rainbow. Happiness was my fatality, my remorse, my worm: my life would always be too enormous to be devoted to strength and to beauty.

Happiness! Its tooth deadly sweet, warned me at the crowing of the cock,—*ad matutinum,* at the *Christus venit,*—in the darkest cities:

O seasons, O castles!
What soul is without sin!

The magic study I've made,
Of happiness none can evade.

To it each time, good luck,
We hear the Gallic cock.

No more desires for me:
It has taken my life in fee.

Charmed body, soul and brain
Delivered of every strain.

O seasons, O castles!

The hour of flight will be
The hour of death for me!

O seasons, O castles!

*

That is over. Now I know how to salute beauty.

Morning

Had I not *once* a lovely youth, heroic, fabulous, to be written on sheets of gold, good luck and to spare! Through what crime, through what fault have I deserved my weakness now? You who declare that beasts sob in their grief, that the sick despair, that the dead have bad dreams, try to relate my fall and my sleep. As for me, I can no more explain myself than the beggar with his endless *Paters* and *Ave Marias. I can no longer speak!*

However, I have finished, I think, the tale of my hell today. It was really hell; the old hell, the one whose doors were opened by the son of man.

From the same desert, in the same night, always my tired eyes awake to the silver star, always, but the Kings of life are not moved, the three magi, mind and heart and soul. When shall we go beyond the mountains and the shores, to greet the birth of new toil, of new wisdom, the flight of tyrants, of demons, the end of superstition, to adore—the first to adore!—Christmas on the earth.

The song of the heavens, the marching of peoples! Slaves, let us not curse life.

FAREWELL

Autumn already!—But why regret an eternal sun if we are embarked on the discovery of divine light—far from all those who fret over seasons.

Autumn. Risen through the motionless mists, our boat turns toward the port of misery, the enormous city with fire-and-mud-stained sky. Ah, the putrid rags, the rain-soaked bread, drunkenness, the thousand loves that have crucified me! Will she never have done, then, that ghoul queen of a million dead souls and dead bodies, *and which will be judged*! I see myself again, skin rotten with mud and pest, worms in my armpits and in my hair, and in my heart much bigger worms, lying among strangers without age, without feeling . . . I might have died there . . . Unbearable evocation! I loathe poverty.

And I dread winter because it is the season of comfort!

Sometimes in the sky I see endless beaches covered with white nations full of joy. Above me a great golden ship waves its multicolored pennants in the breezes of the morning. I created all fêtes, all triumphs, all dramas. I tried to invent new flowers, new stars, new flesh, new tongues. I thought I was acquiring supernatural powers. Well! I must bury my imagination and my memories! An artist's and storyteller's precious fame flung away!

I! I who called myself angel or seer, exempt from all morality, I am returned to the soil with a duty to seek and rough reality to embrace! Peasant!

Am I mistaken? Would charity be the sister of death for me?

At last, I shall ask forgiveness for having fed on lies. And now let's go.

But no friendly hand! And where turn for help!

*

Yes, the new hour is at least very severe.

For I can say that victory is won: the gnashing of teeth, the hissings of fire, the pestilential sighs are abating. All the noisome memories are fading. My last regrets take to their heels,—envy of beggars, brigands, of death's friends, of the backward of all kinds. O damned ones, what if I avenged myself!

One must be absolutely modern.

No hymns! Hold the ground gained. Arduous night! The dried blood smokes on my face, and I have nothing behind me but that horrible bush! . . . Spiritual combat is as brutal as the battle of men: but the vision of justice is the pleasure of God alone.

Meanwhile this is the vigil. Welcome then, all the influx of vigor and real tenderness. And, in the dawn, armed with an ardent patience, we shall enter magnificent cities.

Why talk of a friendly hand! My great advantage is that I can laugh at old lying loves and put to shame those deceitful couples,—I saw the hell of women back there;—and I shall be free to *possess truth in one soul and one body.*

TALE

A Prince was vexed at having devoted himself only to the perfection of ordinary generosities. He foresaw astonishing revolutions of love, and suspected his women of being able to do better than that affable acquiescence set off by heaven and luxuries. He wanted to see the truth, the hour of essential desire and satisfaction. Whether it was an aberration of piety or not, that is what he wanted. Enough worldly power, at least, he had.

All the women who had known him were assassinated: what havoc in the garden of Beauty! At the point of the sword they blessed him. He did not order new ones.—Women re-appeared.

He killed everyone who followed him after the hunt or after the libations.—Everyone followed him.

He amused himself cutting the throats of rare animals. He set palaces in flames. He would rush upon people and hack them to pieces.—Throngs, gilded roofs, beautiful animals still remained.

Can one be in ecstasies over destruction, and through cruelty grow younger! The people did not complain. None opposed him.

One evening he was proudly galloping. A Genie appeared, of an ineffable beauty, unavowable even. In his face and in his bearing shone the promise of a complex and multiple love! of an indescribable happiness, unendurable even! The Prince and the Genie probably annihilated each other in essential health. How could they possibly have helped dying of it? Together then they died.

But the Prince died in his palace at an ordinary age, the Prince was the Genie, the Genie was the Prince.—Skilled music is lacking to our desire.

LIVES

I

O the enormous avenues of the Holy Land, the temple ter-
races! What has become of the Brahman who explained the prov-
erbs to me? Of that time, of that place, I can still see even the old
women! I remember silver hours and sunlight by the rivers, the
hand of the girl on my shoulder, and our caresses standing in the
spicy plains.—A flight of pigeons thunders round my thoughts.
An exile here, I once had a stage on which to play all the master-
pieces of literature. I would show you unheard of riches. I ob-
serve the history of the treasures that you found. I see the sequel.
My wisdom is as scorned as chaos. What is my nothingness to
the stupefaction that awaits you?

II

I am an inventor more deserving far than all those who have
preceded me; a musician, moreover, who has discovered some-
thing like the key of love. At present, a country gentleman of a
lean land with a sober sky, I try to arouse myself with the mem-
ory of my beggar childhood, my apprenticeship or my arrival in
wooden shoes, of polemics, of five or six widowings, and of cer-
tain convivialities when my level head kept me from rising to the
diapason of my comrades. I do not regret my old portion of di-
vine gaiety: the sober air of this acrid country feeds vigorously
my atrocious scepticism. But since this scepticism can not, hence-
forth, be put to use, and since, moreover, I am consecrated to a
new anxiety,—I expect to become a very dangerous madman!

III

In a loft where I was shut up when I was twelve I got to know the world, I illustrated the human comedy. In a wine cellar I learned history. In a northern city, at some nocturnal revel, I met all the women of the old masters. In an ancient arcade of Paris I was taught the classical sciences. In a magnificent dwelling encircled by the entire Orient, I accomplished my prodigious work and spent my illustrious retreat. I have brewed my blood. My duty has been remitted. That is not even to be thought of any longer. I am really from beyond the tomb, and no messages.

DEPARTURE

Seen enough: The vision has been met with in every air.

Had enough. Tumult of cities, in the evening, and in the sun and always.

Known enough. Life's halts.—O Tumults and Visions!

Departure in new affection and new noise.

Morning of Drunkenness

O my Good! O my Beautiful! Atrocious fanfare where I never falter. Rack of enchantments! Hurrah for the unbelievable work and for the marvelous body, for the first time! It began in the midst of children's laughter, with their laughter it will end. This poison will stay in all our veins even when, the fanfares shifting, we shall return to the old inharmony. O now let us, who are so worthy of these tortures! redeem that superhuman promise made to our body and our soul created: that promise, that madness! Elegance, science, violence! They have promised us to bury in darkness the tree of good and evil, to deport tyrannic respectabilities so that we may bring hither our very pure love. It began with a certain disgust—and it ends—unable instantly to grasp this eternity,—it ends with a riot of perfumes.

Laughter of children, discretion of slaves, austerity of virgins, loathing of faces and objects here, holy be all of you in memory of this vigil. It began with every sort of boorishness, behold, it ends with angels of flame and of ice!

Little drunken vigil, holy! if only because of the mask you have bestowed on us. We pronounce you, method! We shall not forget that yesterday you glorified each one of our ages. We have faith in the poison. We know how to give our whole life every day.

The time of the Assassins is here.

VAGABONDS

Pitiful brother! what atrocious vigils I owe him! "I have lacked fervor in this enterprise. I have trifled with his infirmity. My fault should we go back to exile, and to slavery." He thought me unlucky and of a very strange innocence, and would add disquieting reasons.

For reply I would sneer at this Satanic doctor and, in the end, going to the window I would create beyond the countryside crossed by bands of rare music, phantoms of nocturnal luxury to come.

After this vaguely hygienic diversion, I would lie down on my pallet. And almost every night, no sooner asleep than the poor brother would rise, his mouth rotten, eyes starting from his head,—just as he had dreamed he looked!—and would pull me out into the room, howling his dream of imbecilic sorrow.

I had, in truth, taken upon myself in all sincerity, the task of returning him to his primitive state of child of the Sun,—and, nourished by the wine of caverns and the biscuit of the road, we wandered, I impatient to find the place and the formula!

Vigils

I

It is repose in the light, neither fever nor languor, on a bed or on a meadow.

It is the friend neither violent nor weak. The friend.

It is the beloved neither tormenting nor tormented. The beloved.

Air and the world not sought. Life.

—Was it really this?

—And the dream fades.

II

The lighting comes round to the roof-tree again. From the two extremities of the hall—quite ordinary scenery—harmonic elevations join. The wall opposite the watcher is a psychological succession of atmospheric sections, friezes, bands, and of geological accidents. Intense, quick dream of sentimental groups of beings with all possible characters among all possible appearances.

III

The lamps and the rugs of my vigil make the noise of waves in the night along the hull and around the steerage.

The sea of the vigil, like Emily's breasts.

*

The hangings half way up, undergrowth of emerald tinted lace, where dart the vigil doves.

The metal plaque of the black hearth, real suns of seashores: ah! magic wells; only sight of the dawn this time.

IV

You are still at the temptation of St. Anthony. Capers of clipped zeal, grimacings of puerile pride, collapse and terror.

But you will set yourself this task: all harmonic and architectural possibilities will be aroused around your seat. Perfect beings, never dreamed of, will present themselves for your experiments. The curiosity of ancient multitudes and idle luxuries will pensively throng in your vicinity. Your memory and your senses will be simply the nourishment of your creative impulse. As for the world, when you emerge, what will it have become? In any case nothing of what it seems at present.

H

Every monstrosity violates the atrocious gestures of Hortense. Erotic mechanics, her solitude; her lassitude, amorous dynamics. Under childhood's guidance she has been, in numerous ages, the ardent hygiene of all races. Her door is open to misery. There, the morality of living beings is disembodied in her passion or her action.—O terrible shudder of novice loves on the bloody ground and in the transparent hydrogen!—find Hortense.

Democracy

"The flag goes with the foul landscape, and our jargon muffles the drum.

"In great centers we shall aliment the most cynical prostitution, and massacre logical revolts.

"In spicy and drenched lands!—at the service of monstrous exploitations, either industrial or military.

"Farewell here, no matter where. Conscripts of good will, ours will be a ferocious philosophy, ignorant as to science, rabid for comfort; and let the rest of the world croak.

"That's the system. Let's get going!"

GENIE

He is affection and the present since he has made the house open to foamy winter and to the murmur of summer—he who has purified food and drink—he who is the charm of fleeing places and the superhuman delight of stations.—He is affection and the future, love and force whom we, standing among our rages and our boredoms, see passing in the stormy sky and banners of ecstasy.

He is love, perfect measure re-invented, marvelous and unlooked for reason, and eternity: loved instrument of fatal qualities. We all have known the terror of his concession and of ours; O relish of health, the soaring of our faculties, selfish affection and passion for him,—for him who loves us for his infinite life . . .

And we remember him and he has gone on a journey . . . And if Adoration goes, rings, his promise rings: "Away! superstitions, away! those ancient bodies, those couples, and those ages. It is this present epoch that has foundered!"

He will not go away, he will not come down again from any heaven, he will not accomplish the redemption of the angers of women and the gaieties of men and all this Sin: for it is done, he being and being loved.

O his breaths, his heads, his flights: terrible celerity of perfection of forms and of action.
O fecundity of the mind and immensity of the universe!
His body! the dreamed-of release, the shattering of grace crossed by new violence!
His view, his view! all the ancient kneelings and, at his passing, the pains that are lifted.
His day! the abolition of all sonorous and moving afflictions in intenser music.

His step! migrations more vast than the ancient invasions.

O He and we! Pride more compassionate than the lost chari-
ties.

O world and the pure song of new evils!

He has known us all and all of us has loved: take heed this
winter night, from cape to cape, from the tumultuous pole to the
castle, from the crowd to the shore, from look to look, force and
feelings weary, to hail him, to see him and to send him away, and
under the tides and high in the deserts of snow, to follow his
views,—his breaths,—his body,—his day.

YOUTH

I

Sunday

Problems put by, the inevitable descent of heaven and the visit of memories and the assembly of rhythms occupy the house, the head and the world of the spirit.

—A horse scampers off on the suburban track and along tilled fields and woodlands, pierced by the carbonic pest. A miserable woman of drama, somewhere in the world, sighs for improbable desertions. Desperados pine for strife, drunkenness and wounds.—Along the rivers little children stifle their maledictions.

Let us resume our study to the noise of the devouring work that is assembling and rising in the masses.

II

Sonnet

Man of ordinary constitution, was not the flesh a fruit hung in the orchard;—O child days; the body, a treasure to squander;—O to love the peril or the power of Psyche? The earth had slopes fertile in princes and artists, and lineage and race incited you to crimes and mournings: the world, your fortune and your peril. But at present, that labour crowned, you and your calculations,—you and your impatiences—are nothing but your dance and your voice, not fixed and never forced, although of a double consequence of invention and achievement, a cause,—in a fraternal and discreet humanity through an imageless universe;—might and right reflect your dance and your voice, only appreciated at present.

III

Twenty Years Old

Instructive voices exiled . . . Physical candor bitterly quelled . . .—Adagio.—Ah! the infinite egoism of adolescence, the studious optimism: how the world was full of flowers that summer! Airs and forms dying . . .—A choir to calm impotence and absence! A choir of glasses, of nocturnal melodies . . . Quickly, indeed, the nerves take up the chase.

IV

War

When a child, certain skies refined my vision: all the signs modified my physiognomy. The Phenomena were aroused.—At present, the eternal inflection of moments and the infinity of mathematics drives me through the world, where I endure every civil success, respected by strange childhood and enormous affections.—I dream of a war of right and of might, of a quite unforeseen logic.

It is as simple as a musical phrase.

SALE

For sale what the Jews have not sold, what neither nobility nor crime have tasted, what is unknown to execrable love and to the infernal probity of the masses! what neither time nor science need recognize:

Reconstituted Voices; fraternal awakening of all choral and orchestral energies and their instantaneous application; the opportunity, the only one, for the deliverance of our senses!

For sale Bodies without price, outside any race, any world, any sex, any lineage! Riches gushing at every step! Uncontrolled sale of diamonds!

For sale anarchy for the masses; irresistible satisfaction for rare connoisseurs; atrocious death for the faithful and for lovers!

For sale habitations and migrations, sports, enchantments and unparalleled comforts, and the noise and the movement and the future that they make!

For sale the fruits of calculation and the incredible soarings of harmony. Amazing discoveries, and terms never dreamed of,— immediate possession.

Insensate and infinite flight toward invisible splendours, toward immaterial delights—and its maddening secrets for every vice—and its gaiety, terrifying to the mob.

For sale, the bodies, the voices, the enormous and incontestable wealth—that which will never be sold. Salesmen are not at the end of their bargains! No danger that travelers will be called to account in a hurry.

The Deserts of Love

FOREWORD

These are the writings of a young, a very young man, who has grown up anywhere; without mother, without country, indifferent to everything other people know, fleeing all moral courage, like many other pitiful young men before him. But he, so full of anxiety and so troubled, did nothing but set his course toward death as toward a terrible and fatal decency. Not having loved women,—fullblooded though he was!—his soul and his heart, all his strength, were taken up with aberrations, strange and sad. The following dreams,—his loves!—that came to him in his beds and in the streets, and from their sequence and from their ending sweet religious considerations may arise. Who will recall the continuous sleep of the legendary Mohammedans,—brave though and circumcised! But this fantastic suffering possessing a disturbing sovereignty, it is sincerely to be hoped that this Soul, among us lost, and who desires death, it seems, should meet at that instant authentic consolations and be worthy.

I

This time it is the Woman whom I saw in the City, and to whom I have spoken and who speaks to me.

I was in a room without light. They came to tell me she was there; and I saw her in my bed, all mine, without light! I was troubled, and largely because it was my parents' house, so anguish filled me! I was in rags while she, a woman of the world, was giving herself to me: she would have to go away! A nameless anguish: I took her, and let her fall from the bed, almost naked; and, in my unutterable weakness, I fell upon her and rolled with her on the rugs, without light! The family lamp reddened one by one the adjoining rooms. Then, the woman disappeared. I shed more tears than God could ever have required.

I went out into the city without end. O weariness! Drowned in the insensible night and in the flight of happiness. It was like a winter night with a fall of snow to smother the world once and for all. The friends to whom I cried: Where is she? falsely replied. I was there in front of the windows where she goes every evening. I was running through a buried garden. They drove me away. At all this I wept prodigiously. Finally, I went down into a place filled with dust and, sitting on some lumber, I drained my body of all its tears that night.—And yet always my exhaustion returned.

I understood that She belonged to her everyday life; and that it would take longer for the turn of kindness to come again than for the reproduction of a star. She has not returned and will never return, the Adorable One, who visited me in my home,—something I should never have presumed to ask. True, this time, I wept more than all the children in the world.

II

It is certainly the same countryside. The same rustic house of my parents: even the same room where the overdoors are russet sheepfolds with lions and coats of arms. At dinner, there is a room with candles and wines and antique paneling. The dining table is very large. The servants! there were several as far as I can remember.—One of my young friends of old was there, a priest and dressed like a priest; at present: for the sake of greater freedom. I remember his purple room with yellow paper panes; and his hidden books that had soaked in the sea!

As for me, I was abandoned in that country house without end; reading in the kitchen, drying the mud off my clothes in front of the guests with their drawing-room conversation: mortally troubled by the murmur of the milk of morning and the night of the last century.

I was in a very dark room: what was I doing? A little servant girl came toward me: a puppy I should say: notwithstanding she was beautiful, noble and maternal beyond words to me: pure, familiar, altogether charming. She pinched my arm.

I can no longer remember even her face very well: much less her arm whose flesh I rolled between my fingers; nor her mouth which mine seized like a desperate little wave endlessly lapping. I flung her onto a basket of cushions and sail cloth in a dark corner. And I remember nothing but her white drawers trimmed with lace.

Then, O despair! The wall became dimly the shadow of trees, and I was plunged in the amorous sadness of the night.

The Drunken Boat

As I came down the impassable Rivers,
I felt no more the bargemen's guiding hands,
Targets for yelling red-skins they were nailed
Naked to painted poles.

What did I care for any crews,
Carriers of English cotton or of Flemish grain!
Bargemen and all that hubbub left behind,
The waters let me go my own free way.

In the furious lashings of the tides,
Emptier than children's minds, I through that winter
Ran! And great peninsulas unmoored
Never knew more triumphant uproar than I knew.

The tempest blessed my wakings on the sea.
Light as a cork I danced upon the waves,
Eternal rollers of the deep sunk dead,
Nor missed at night the lanterns' idiot eyes!

Sweeter than sour apples to a child,
Green waters seeped through all my seams,
Washing the stains of vomit and blue wine,
And swept away my anchor and my helm.

And since then I've been bathing in the Poem
Of star-infused and milky Sea,
Devouring the azure greens, where, flotsam pale,
A brooding corpse at times drifts by;

Where, dyeing suddenly the blue,
Rhythms delirious and slow in the blaze of day,

Stronger than alcohol, vaster than your lyres,
Ferment the bitter reds of love!

I know the lightning-opened skies, waterspouts,
Eddies and surfs; I know the night,
And dawn arisen like a colony of doves,
And sometimes I have seen what men have thought they saw!

I've seen the low sun, fearful with mystic signs,
Lighting with far flung violet arms,
Like actors in an ancient tragedy,
The fluted waters shivering far away.

I've dreamed green nights of dazzling snows,
Slow kisses on the eyelids of the sea,
The terrible flow of unforgettable saps,
And singing phosphors waking yellow and blue.

Months through I've followed the assaulting tides
Like maddened cattle leaping up the reefs,
Nor ever thought the Marys' luminous feet
Could curb the muzzle of the panting Deep.

I've touched, you know, fantastic Floridas
Mingling the eyes of panthers, human-skinned, with flowers!
And rainbows stretched like endless reins
To glaucous flocks beneath the seas.

I've seen fermenting marshes like enormous nets
Where in the reeds a whole Leviathan decays!
Crashings of waters in the midst of calms!
Horizons toward far chasms cataracting!

Glaciers and silver suns, fiery skies and pearly seas,
Hideous wrecks at the bottom of brown gulfs
Where giant serpents vermin ridden
Drop with black perfumes from the twisted trees!

I would show children those dorados,
And golden singing fishes in blue seas.
Foam flowers have blest my aimless wanderings,
Ineffable winds have given me wings.

Tired of poles and zones, sometimes the martyred sea,
Rolling me gently on her sobbing breast,
Lifted her shadow flowers with yellow cups toward me
And I stayed there like a woman on her knees.

Island, I sailed, and on my gunnels tossed
Quarrels and droppings of the pale-eyed birds,
While floating slowly past my fragile bands,
Backward the drowned went dreaming by.

But I, lost boat in the cove's trailing tresses,
Tossed by the tempest into birdless space,
Whose water-drunken carcass never would have salvaged
Old Monitor or Galleon of the Hanseatic League;

Who, ridden by violet mists, steaming and free,
Pierced the sky reddening like a wall,
Covered with lichens of the sun and azure's phlem,
Preserves that all good poets love,

Who, spotted with electric crescents ran,
Mad plank with escort of black hypocamps,
While Augusts with their hammer blows tore down
The sea-blue, spiral-flaming skies;

Who trembling felt Behemoth's rut
And Maelstroms groaning fifty leagues away,
Eternal scudder through the quiescent blue,
I long for Europe's parapets!

I've seen sidereal archipelagos! Islands
Whose delirious skies open for wanderers:

"Is it in such bottomless nights you sleep, exiled,
O countless golden birds, O Force to come?"

True I have wept too much! Dawns are heartbreaking;
Cruel all moons and bitter the suns.
Drunk with love's acrid torpors,
O let my keel burst! Let me go to the sea!

If I desire any European water, it's the black pond
And cold, where toward perfumed evening
A sad child on his knees sets sail
A boat as frail as a May butterfly.

I can no longer, bathed in your languors, O waves,
Obliterate the cotton carriers' wake,
Nor cross the pride of pennants and of flags,
Nor swim past prison hulks' hateful eyes!

W. B. Yeats

Once out of nature I shall never take
My bodily form from any natural thing,
But such a form as Grecian goldsmiths make
Of hammered gold and gold enamelling
To keep a drowsy Emperor awake;
Or set upon a golden bough to sing
To lords and ladies of Byzantium
Of what is past, or passing, or to come.

"Sailing to Byzantium"

W. B. Yeats

(Ireland, 1865–1939)

For most readers of twentieth-century poetry, William Butler Yeats is the figure most revered. T. S. Eliot called Yeats "the greatest [poet] in this language, and so far as I am able to judge, in any language." He has been the model—or at the very least an inevitable presence—for the century of poets who followed him.

Yeats was born in Dublin, the son of John Butler Yeats, a respected portrait painter. At first the young Yeats, too, intended to become a painter, and he attended a Dublin art school. But he soon turned to a number of other interests. Avid for revelation of every sort, Yeats gravitated toward the occult and joined the recently formed Theosophical Society. Intrigued by William Blake's visions, he devoted much time to the first complete edition of the poet's works. Yeats also became interested in the poetry and philosophy of the Hindu Upanishads and translated the work of the Indian poet Rabindranath Tagore. Identifying early Irish folktales and stories as a source of spiritual and poetic inspiration—as well as one basis for the establishment of an Irish cultural and national identity that would concern him all his life—Yeats published an edition of folktales that is still widely used.

Yeats's early poetic efforts aimed for a self-sufficient universe of interlocking symbols. "I am very religious," he once wrote, "and deprived by Huxley and Tyndall, whom I detested, of the simple-minded religion of my childhood, I had made a new religion, almost an infallible church of poetic tradition."

In 1889 he met the woman who would inform and haunt his poetry for the rest of his life—Maud Gonne, a beautiful Irish activist. She agreed to a mystical marriage with him, but when he attempted to formalize it in this world, she turned him down. He later fell in love with Gonne's daughter Iseult, but she, too, rejected Yeats's offer of marriage.

In 1904, with the help of the formidable Lady Gregory, Yeats founded the Abbey Theatre in Dublin, where he staged his own plays as well as those of other writers. Although the theater played an important part in the cultural life of Ireland, it took Yeats away from his poetry for some time.

Still feeling the need to marry, in 1917, with some trepidation, he wed the young Georgie Hyde-lees. Soon afterward he felt entirely confirmed in his choice, for it turned out that his wife was possessed by a gift for automatic writing. The communications she received grew to thousands of pages of philosophy and images, the essence of which were fundamental to the elaborate symbology of Yeats's *A Vision*, published in 1925.

He committed to yet another form of devotion to his country when, in 1923, after the creation of the Irish Free State, he became a senator for six years. Yeats never abandoned his visions of unity—poetic, cultural, philosophical, and national—yet he believed that art should lead back to real life, and make it sacred. We witness in his poetry a constant wavering between the flesh and the spirit, the material world and the spiritual—quite brilliantly expressed in his poem "A Dialogue of Self and Soul," in which we find these lines:

> The folly that man does
> Or must suffer, if he woos
> A proud woman not kindred of his soul.

THE LAKE ISLE OF INNISFREE

I will arise and go now, and go to Innisfree,
And a small cabin build there, of clay and wattles made:
Nine bean-rows will I have there, a hive for the honey-bee,
And live alone in the bee-loud glade.

And I shall have some peace there, for peace comes dropping
  slow,
Dropping from the veils of the morning to where the cricket
  sings;
There midnight's all a glimmer, and noon a purple glow,
And evening full of the linnet's wings.

I will arise and go now, for always night and day
I hear lake water lapping with low sounds by the shore;
While I stand on the roadway, or on the pavements grey,
I hear it in the deep heart's core.

The Cloak, the Boat, and the Shoes

'What do you make so fair and bright?'

'I make the cloak of Sorrow:
O lovely to see in all men's sight
Shall be the cloak of Sorrow,
In all men's sight.'

'What do you build with sails for flight?'

'I build a boat for Sorrow:
O swift on the seas all day and night
Saileth the rover Sorrow,
All day and night.'

'What do you weave with wool so white?'

'I weave the shoes of Sorrow:
Soundless shall be the footfall light
In all men's ears of Sorrow,
Sudden and light.'

THE SONG OF WANDERING AENGUS

I went out to the hazel wood,
Because a fire was in my head,
And cut and peeled a hazel wand,
And hooked a berry to a thread;
And when white moths were on the wing,
And moth-like stars were flickering out,
I dropped the berry in a stream
And caught a little silver trout.

When I had laid it on the floor
I went to blow the fire aflame,
But something rustled on the floor,
And some one called me by my name:
It had become a glimmering girl
With apple blossom in her hair
Who called me by my name and ran
And faded through the brightening air.

Though I am old with wandering
Through hollow lands and hilly lands,
I will find out where she has gone,
And kiss her lips and take her hands;
And walk among long dappled grass,
And pluck till time and times are done
The silver apples of the moon,
The golden apples of the sun.

THE OLD MEN ADMIRING THEMSELVES IN THE WATER

I heard the old, old men say,
'Everything alters,
And one by one we drop away.'
They had hands like claws, and their knees
Were twisted like the old thorn-trees
By the waters.
I heard the old, old men say,
'All that's beautiful drifts away
Like the waters.'

The Three Hermits

Three old hermits took the air
By a cold and desolate sea,
First was muttering a prayer,
Second rummaged for a flea;
On a windy stone, the third,
Giddy with his hundredth year,
Sang unnoticed like a bird:
'Though the Door of Death is near
And what waits behind the door,
Three times in a single day
I, though upright on the shore,
Fall asleep when I should pray.'
So the first, but now the second:
'We're but given what we have earned
When all thoughts and deeds are reckoned,
So it's plain to be discerned
That the shades of holy men
Who have failed, being weak of will,
Pass the Door of Birth again,
And are plagued by crowds, until
They've the passion to escape.'
Moaned the other, 'They are thrown
Into some most fearful shape.'
But the second mocked his moan:
'They are not changed to anything,
Having loved God once, but maybe
To a poet or a king
Or a witty lovely lady.'
While he'd rummaged rags and hair,
Caught and cracked his flea, the third,
Giddy with his hundredth year,
Sang unnoticed like a bird.

A COAT

I made my song a coat
Covered with embroideries
Out of old mythologies
From heel to throat;
But the fools caught it,
Wore it in the world's eyes
As though they'd wrought it.
Song, let them take it,
For there's more enterprise
In walking naked.

The Wild Swans at Coole

The trees are in their autumn beauty,
The woodland paths are dry,
Under the October twilight the water
Mirrors a still sky;
Upon the brimming water among the stones
Are nine-and-fifty swans.

The nineteenth autumn has come upon me
Since I first made my count;
I saw, before I had well finished,
All suddenly mount
And scatter wheeling in great broken rings
Upon their clamorous wings.

I have looked upon those brilliant creatures,
And now my heart is sore.
All's changed since I, hearing at twilight,
The first time on this shore,
The bell-beat of their wings above my head,
Trod with a lighter tread.

Unwearied still, lover by lover,
They paddle in the cold
Companionable streams or climb the air;
Their hearts have not grown old;
Passion or conquest, wander where they will,
Attend upon them still.

But now they drift on the still water,
Mysterious, beautiful;

Among what rushes will they build,
By what lake's edge or pool
Delight men's eyes when I awake some day
To find they have flown away?

MEMORY

One had a lovely face,
And two or three had charm,
But charm and face were in vain
Because the mountain grass
Cannot but keep the form
Where the mountain hare has lain.

EASTER, 1916

I have met them at close of day
Coming with vivid faces
From counter or desk among grey
Eighteenth-century houses.
I have passed with a nod of the head
Or polite meaningless words,
Or have lingered awhile and said
Polite meaningless words,
And thought before I had done
Of a mocking tale or a gibe
To please a companion
Around the fire at the club,
Being certain that they and I
But lived where motley is worn:
All changed, changed utterly:
A terrible beauty is born.

That woman's days were spent
In ignorant good-will,
Her nights in argument
Until her voice grew shrill.
What voice more sweet than hers
When, young and beautiful,
She rode to harriers?
This man had kept a school
And rode our wingèd horse;
This other his helper and friend
Was coming into his force;
He might have won fame in the end,
So sensitive his nature seemed,
So daring and sweet his thought.
This other man I had dreamed

A drunken, vainglorious lout.
He had done most bitter wrong
To some who are near my heart,
Yet I number him in the song;
He, too, has resigned his part
In the casual comedy;
He, too, has been changed in his turn,
Transformed utterly:
A terrible beauty is born.

Hearts with one purpose alone
Through summer and winter seem
Enchanted to a stone
To trouble the living stream.
The horse that comes from the road,
The rider, the birds that range
From cloud to tumbling cloud,
Minute by minute they change;
A shadow of cloud on the stream
Changes minute by minute;
A horse-hoof slides on the brim,
And a horse plashes within it;
The long-legged moor-hens dive,
And hens to moor-cocks call;
Minute by minute they live:
The stone's in the midst of all.

Too long a sacrifice
Can make a stone of the heart.
O when may it suffice?
That is Heaven's part, our part
To murmur name upon name,
As a mother names her child
When sleep at last has come
On limbs that had run wild.
What is it but nightfall?
No, no, not night but death;

Was it needless death after all?
For England may keep faith
For all that is done and said.
We know their dream; enough
To know they dreamed and are dead;
And what if excess of love
Bewildered them till they died?
I write it out in a verse—
MacDonagh and MacBride
And Connolly and Pearse
Now and in time to be,
Wherever green is worn,
Are changed, changed utterly:
A terrible beauty is born.

THE SECOND COMING

Turning and turning in the widening gyre
The falcon cannot hear the falconer;
Things fall apart; the centre cannot hold;
Mere anarchy is loosed upon the world,
The blood-dimmed tide is loosed, and everywhere
The ceremony of innocence is drowned;
The best lack all conviction, while the worst
Are full of passionate intensity.

Surely some revelation is at hand;
Surely the Second Coming is at hand.
The Second Coming! Hardly are those words out
When a vast image out of *Spiritus Mundi*
Troubles my sight: somewhere in sands of the desert
A shape with lion body and the head of a man,
A gaze blank and pitiless as the sun,
Is moving its slow thighs, while all about it
Reel shadows of the indignant desert birds.
The darkness drops again; but now I know
That twenty centuries of stony sleep
Were vexed to nightmare by a rocking cradle,
And what rough beast, its hour come round at last,
Slouches towards Bethlehem to be born?

Sailing to Byzantium

I

That is no country for old men. The young
In one another's arms, birds in the trees
—Those dying generations—at their song,
The salmon-falls, the mackerel-crowded seas,
Fish, flesh, or fowl, commend all summer long
Whatever is begotten, born, and dies.
Caught in that sensual music all neglect
Monuments of unageing intellect.

II

An aged man is but a paltry thing,
A tattered coat upon a stick, unless
Soul clap its hands and sing, and louder sing
For every tatter in its mortal dress,
Nor is there singing school but studying
Monuments of its own magnificence;
And therefore I have sailed the seas and come
To the holy city of Byzantium.

III

O sages standing in God's holy fire
As in the gold mosaic of a wall,
Come from the holy fire, perne in a gyre,
And be the singing-masters of my soul.
Consume my heart away; sick with desire
And fastened to a dying animal
It knows not what it is; and gather me
Into the artifice of eternity.

IV

Once out of nature I shall never take
My bodily form from any natural thing,
But such a form as Grecian goldsmiths make
Of hammered gold and gold enamelling
To keep a drowsy Emperor awake;
Or set upon a golden bough to sing
To lords and ladies of Byzantium
Of what is past, or passing, or to come.

THE TOWER

I

What shall I do with this absurdity—
O heart, O troubled heart—this caricature,
Decrepit age that has been tied to me
As to a dog's tail?
                        Never had I more
Excited, passionate, fantastical
Imagination, nor an ear and eye
That more expected the impossible—
No, not in boyhood when with rod and fly,
Or the humbler worm, I climbed Ben Bulben's back
And had the livelong summer day to spend.
It seems that I must bid the Muse go pack,
Choose Plato and Plotinus for a friend
Until imagination, ear and eye,
Can be content with argument and deal
In abstract things; or be derided by
A sort of battered kettle at the heel.

II

I pace upon the battlements and stare
On the foundations of a house, or where
Tree, like a sooty finger, starts from the earth;
And send imagination forth
Under the day's declining beam, and call
Images and memories
From ruin or from ancient trees,
For I would ask a question of them all.

Beyond the ridge lived Mrs. French, and once
When every silver candlestick or sconce

Lit up the dark mahogany and the wine,
A serving-man, that could divine
That most respected lady's every wish,
Ran and with the garden shears
Clipped an insolent farmer's ears
And brought them in a little covered dish.

Some few remembered still when I was young
A peasant girl commended by a song,
Who'd lived somewhere upon that rocky place,
And praised the colour of her face,
And had the greater joy in praising her,
Remembering that, if walked she there,
Farmers jostled at the fair
So great a glory did the song confer.

And certain men, being maddened by those rhymes,
Or else by toasting her a score of times,
Rose from the table and declared it right
To test their fancy by their sight;
But they mistook the brightness of the moon
For the prosaic light of day—
Music had driven their wits astray—
And one was drowned in the great bog of Cloone.

Strange, but the man who made the song was blind;
Yet, now I have considered it, I find
That nothing strange; the tragedy began
With Homer that was a blind man,
And Helen has all living hearts betrayed.
O may the moon and sunlight seem
One inextricable beam,
For if I triumph I must make men mad.

And I myself created Hanrahan
And drove him drunk or sober through the dawn
From somewhere in the neighbouring cottages.
Caught by an old man's juggleries
He stumbled, tumbled, fumbled to and fro

And had but broken knees for hire
And horrible splendour of desire;
I thought it all out twenty years ago:

Good fellows shuffled cards in an old bawn;
And when that ancient ruffian's turn was on
He so bewitched the cards under his thumb
That all but the one card became
A pack of hounds and not a pack of cards,
And that he changed into a hare.
Hanrahan rose in a frenzy there
And followed up those baying creatures towards—

O towards I have forgotten what—enough!
I must recall a man that neither love
Nor music nor an enemy's clipped ear
Could, he was so harried, cheer;
A figure that has grown so fabulous
There's not a neighbour left to say
When he finished his dog's day:
An ancient bankrupt master of this house.

Before that ruin came, for centuries,
Rough men-at-arms, cross-gartered to the knees
Or shod in iron, climbed the narrow stairs,
And certain men-at-arms there were
Whose images, in the Great Memory stored,
Come with loud cry and panting breast
To break upon a sleeper's rest
While their great wooden dice beat on the board.

As I would question all, come all who can;
Come old, necessitous, half-mounted man;
And bring beauty's blind rambling celebrant;
The red man the juggler sent
Through God-forsaken meadows; Mrs. French,
Gifted with so fine an ear;

The man drowned in a bog's mire,
When mocking Muses chose the country wench.

Did all old men and women, rich and poor,
Who trod upon these rocks or passed this door,
Whether in public or in secret rage
As I do now against old age?
But I have found an answer in those eyes
That are impatient to be gone;
Go therefore; but leave Hanrahan,
For I need all his mighty memories.

Old lecher with a love on every wind,
Bring up out of that deep considering mind
All that you have discovered in the grave,
For it is certain that you have
Reckoned up every unforeknown, unseeing
Plunge, lured by a softening eye,
Or by a touch or a sigh,
Into the labyrinth of another's being;

Does the imagination dwell the most
Upon a woman won or woman lost?
If on the lost, admit you turned aside
From a great labyrinth out of pride,
Cowardice, some silly over-subtle thought
Or anything called conscience once;
And that if memory recur, the sun's
Under eclipse and the day blotted out.

III

It is time that I wrote my will;
I choose upstanding men
That climb the streams until
The fountain leap, and at dawn
Drop their cast at the side

Of dripping stone; I declare
They shall inherit my pride,
The pride of people that were
Bound neither to Cause nor to State,
Neither to slaves that were spat on,
Nor to the tyrants that spat,
The people of Burke and of Grattan
That gave, though free to refuse—
Pride, like that of the morn,
When the headlong light is loose,
Or that of the fabulous horn,
Or that of the sudden shower
When all streams are dry,
Or that of the hour
When the swan must fix his eye
Upon a fading gleam,
Float out upon a long
Last reach of glittering stream
And there sing his last song.
And I declare my faith:
I mock Plotinus' thought
And cry in Plato's teeth,
Death and life were not
Till man made up the whole,
Made lock, stock and barrel
Out of his bitter soul,
Aye, sun and moon and star, all,
And further add to that
That, being dead, we rise,
Dream and so create
Translunar Paradise.
I have prepared my peace
With learned Italian things
And the proud stones of Greece,
Poet's imaginings
And memories of love,
Memories of the words of women,
All those things whereof

Man makes a superhuman
Mirror-resembling dream.

As at the loophole there
The daws chatter and scream,
And drop twigs layer upon layer.
When they have mounted up,
The mother bird will rest
On their hollow top,
And so warm her wild nest.

I leave both faith and pride
To young upstanding men
Climbing the mountain side,
That under bursting dawn
They may drop a fly;
Being of that metal made
Till it was broken by
This sedentary trade.

Now shall I make my soul,
Compelling it to study
In a learned school
Till the wreck of body,
Slow decay of blood,
Testy delirium
Or dull decrepitude,
Or what worse evil come—
The death of friends, or death
Of every brilliant eye
That made a catch in the breath—
Seem but the clouds of the sky
When the horizon fades;
Or a bird's sleepy cry
Among the deepening shades.

ALL SOULS' NIGHT

Epilogue to 'A Vision'

Midnight has come, and the great Christ Church Bell
And many a lesser bell sound through the room;
And it is All Souls' Night,
And two long glasses brimmed with muscatel
Bubble upon the table. A ghost may come;
For it is a ghost's right,
His element is so fine
Being sharpened by his death,
To drink from the wine-breath
While our gross palates drink from the whole wine,

I need some mind that, if the cannon sound
From every quarter of the world, can stay
Wound in mind's pondering
As mummies in the mummy-cloth are wound;
Because I have a marvellous thing to say,
A certain marvellous thing
None but the living mock,
Though not for sober ear;
It may be all that hear
Should laugh and weep an hour upon the clock.

Horton's the first I call. He loved strange thought
And knew that sweet extremity of pride
That's called platonic love,
And that to such a pitch of passion wrought
Nothing could bring him, when his lady died,
Anodyne for his love.
Words were but wasted breath;
One dear hope had he:
The inclemency
Of that or the next winter would be death.

Two thoughts were so mixed up I could not tell
Whether of her or God he thought the most,
But think that his mind's eye,
When upward turned, on one sole image fell;
And that a slight companionable ghost,
Wild with divinity,
Had so lit up the whole
Immense miraculous house
The Bible promised us,
It seemed a gold-fish swimming in a bowl.

On Florence Emery I call the next,
Who finding the first wrinkles on a face
Admired and beautiful,
And by foreknowledge of the future vexed;
Diminished beauty, multiplied commonplace;
Preferred to teach a school
Away from neighbour or friend,
Among dark skins, and there
Permit foul years to wear
Hidden from eyesight to the unnoticed end.

Before that end much had she ravelled out
From a discourse in figurative speech
By some learned Indian
On the soul's journey. How it is whirled about,
Wherever the orbit of the moon can reach,
Until it plunge into the sun;
And there, free and yet fast,
Being both Chance and Choice,
Forget its broken toys
And sink into its own delight at last.

I call MacGregor Mathers from his grave,
For in my first hard spring-time we were friends,
Although of late estranged.
I thought him half a lunatic, half knave,
And told him so, but friendship never ends;
And what if mind seem changed,

And it seem changed with the mind,
When thoughts rise up unbid
On generous things that he did
And I grow half contented to be blind!

He had much industry at setting out,
Much boisterous courage, before loneliness
Had driven him crazed;
For meditations upon unknown thought
Make human intercourse grow less and less;
They are neither paid nor praised.
But he'd object to the host,
The glass because my glass;
A ghost-lover he was
And may have grown more arrogant being a ghost.

But names are nothing. What matter who it be,
So that his elements have grown so fine
The fume of muscatel
Can give his sharpened palate ecstasy
No living man can drink from the whole wine.
I have mummy truths to tell
Whereat the living mock,
Though not for sober ear,
For maybe all that hear
Should laugh and weep an hour upon the clock.

Such thought—such thought have I that hold it tight
Till meditation master all its parts,
Nothing can stay my glance
Until that glance run in the world's despite
To where the damned have howled away their hearts,
And where the blessed dance;
Such thought, that in it bound
I need no other thing,
Would in mind's wandering
As mummies in the mummy-cloth are wound.

LEDA AND THE SWAN

A sudden blow: the great wings beating still
Above the staggering girl, her thighs caressed
By the dark webs, her nape caught in his bill,
He holds her helpless breast upon his breast.

How can those terrified vague fingers push
The feathered glory from her loosening thighs?
And how can body, laid in that white rush,
But feel the strange heart beating where it lies?

A shudder in the loins engenders there
The broken wall, the burning roof and tower
And Agamemnon dead.
                              Being so caught up,
So mastered by the brute blood of the air,
Did she put on his knowledge with his power
Before the indifferent beak could let her drop?

AMONG SCHOOL CHILDREN

I

I walk through the long schoolroom questioning;
A kind old nun in a white hood replies;
The children learn to cipher and to sing,
To study reading-books and history,
To cut and sew, be neat in everything
In the best modern way—the children's eyes
In momentary wonder stare upon
A sixty-year-old smiling public man.

II

I dream of a Ledaean body, bent
Above a sinking fire, a tale that she
Told of a harsh reproof, or trivial event
That changed some childish day to tragedy—
Told, and it seemed that our two natures blent
Into a sphere from youthful sympathy,
Or else, to alter Plato's parable,
Into the yolk and white of the one shell.

III

And thinking of that fit of grief or rage
I look upon one child or t'other there
And wonder if she stood so at that age—
For even daughters of the swan can share
Something of every paddler's heritage—
And had that colour upon cheek or hair,

And thereupon my heart is driven wild:
She stands before me as a living child.

IV

Her present image floats into the mind—
Did Quattrocento finger fashion it
Hollow of cheek as though it drank the wind
And took a mess of shadows for its meat?
And I though never of Ledaean kind
Had pretty plumage once—enough of that,
Better to smile on all that smile, and show
There is a comfortable kind of old scarecrow.

V

What youthful mother, a shape upon her lap
Honey of generation had betrayed,
And that must sleep, shriek, struggle to escape
As recollection or the drug decide,
Would think her son, did she but see that shape
With sixty or more winters on its head,
A compensation for the pang of his birth,
Or the uncertainty of his setting forth?

VI

Plato thought nature but a spume that plays
Upon a ghostly paradigm of things;
Solider Aristotle played the taws
Upon the bottom of a king of kings;
World-famous golden-thighed Pythagoras
Fingered upon a fiddle-stick or strings
What a star sang and careless Muses heard:
Old clothes upon old sticks to scare a bird.

VII

Both nuns and mothers worship images,
But those the candles light are not as those
That animate a mother's reveries,
But keep a marble or a bronze repose.
And yet they too break hearts—O Presences
That passion, piety or affection knows,
And that all heavenly glory symbolise—
O self-born mockers of man's enterprise;

VIII

Labour is blossoming or dancing where
The body is not bruised to pleasure soul,
Nor beauty born out of its own despair,
Nor blear-eyed wisdom out of midnight oil.
O chestnut tree, great rooted blossomer,
Are you the leaf, the blossom or the bole?
O body swayed to music, O brightening glance,
How can we know the dancer from the dance?

A Dialogue of Self and Soul

My Soul. I summon to the winding ancient stair;
　　Set all your mind upon the steep ascent,
　　Upon the broken, crumbling battlement,
　　Upon the breathless starlit air,
　　Upon the star that marks the hidden pole;
　　Fix every wandering thought upon
　　That quarter where all thought is done:
　　Who can distinguish darkness from the soul?

My Self. The consecrated blade upon my knees
　　Is Sato's ancient blade, still as it was,
　　Still razor-keen, still like a looking-glass
　　Unspotted by the centuries;
　　That flowering, silken, old embroidery, torn
　　From some court-lady's dress and round
　　The wooden scabbard bound and wound,
　　Can, tattered, still protect, faded adorn.

My Soul. Why should the imagination of a man
　　Long past his prime remember things that are
　　Emblematical of love and war?
　　Think of ancestral night that can,
　　If but imagination scorn the earth
　　And intellect its wandering
　　To this and that and t'other thing,
　　Deliver from the crime of death and birth.

My Self. Montashigi, third of his family, fashioned it
　　Five hundred years ago, about it lie
　　Flowers from I know not what embroidery—

Heart's purple—and all these I set
For emblems of the day against the tower
Emblematical of the night,
And claim as by a soldier's right
A charter to commit the crime once more.

My Soul. Such fullness in that quarter overflows
And falls into the basin of the mind
That man is stricken deaf and dumb and blind,
For intellect no longer knows
Is from the *Ought,* or *Knower* from the *Known*—
That is to say, ascends to Heaven;
Only the dead can be forgiven;
But when I think of that my tongue's a stone.

II

My Self. A living man is blind and drinks his drop.
What matter if the ditches are impure?
What matter if I live it all once more?
Endure that toil of growing up;
The ignominy of boyhood; the distress
Of boyhood changing into man;
The unfinished man and his pain
Brought face to face with his own clumsiness;

The finished man among his enemies?—
How in the name of Heaven can he escape
That defiling and disfigured shape
The mirror of malicious eyes
Casts upon his eyes until at last
He thinks that shape must be his shape?
And what's the good of an escape
If honour find him in the wintry blast?

I am content to live it all again
And yet again, if it be life to pitch
Into the frog-spawn of a blind man's ditch,

A blind man battering blind men;
Or into that most fecund ditch of all,
The folly that man does
Or must suffer, if he woos
A proud woman not kindred of his soul.

I am content to follow to its source
Every event in action or in thought;
Measure the lot; forgive myself the lot!
When such as I cast out remorse
So great a sweetness flows into the breast
We must laugh and we must sing,
We are blest by everything,
Everything we look upon is blest.

Lapis Lazuli

(For Harry Clifton)

I have heard that hysterical women say
They are sick of the palette and fiddle-bow,
Of poets that are always gay,
For everybody knows or else should know
That if nothing drastic is done
Aeroplane and Zeppelin will come out,
Pitch like King Billy bomb-balls in
Until the town lie beaten flat.

All perform their tragic play,
There struts Hamlet, there is Lear,
That's Ophelia, that Cordelia;
Yet they, should the last scene be there,
The great stage curtain about to drop,
If worthy their prominent part in the play,
Do not break up their lines to weep.
They know that Hamlet and Lear are gay;
Gaiety transfiguring all that dread.
All men have aimed at, found and lost;
Black out; Heaven blazing into the head:
Tragedy wrought to its uttermost.
Though Hamlet rambles and Lear rages,
And all the drop-scenes drop at once
Upon a hundred thousand stages,
It cannot grow by an inch or an ounce.

On their own feet they came, or on shipboard,
Camel-back, horse-back, ass-back, mule-back,
Old civilisations put to the sword.
Then they and their wisdom went to rack:

No handiwork of Callimachus,
Who handled marble as if it were bronze,
Made draperies that seemed to rise
When sea-wind swept the corner, stands;
His long lamp chimney shaped like the stem
Of a slender palm, stood but a day;
All things fall and are built again
And those that build them again are gay.

Two Chinamen, behind them a third,
Are carved in Lapis Lazuli,
Over them flies a long-legged bird,
A symbol of longevity;
The third, doubtless a serving-man,
Carries a musical instrument.

Every discoloration of the stone,
Every accidental crack or dent,
Seems a water-course or an avalanche,
Or lofty slope where it still snows
Though doubtless plum or cherry-branch
Sweetens the little half-way house
Those Chinamen climb towards, and I
Delight to imagine them seated there;
There, on the mountain and the sky,
On all the tragic scene they stare.
One asks for mournful melodies;
Accomplished fingers begin to play.
Their eyes mid many wrinkles, their eyes,
Their ancient, glittering eyes, are gay.

Under Ben Bulben

I

Swear by what the Sages spoke
Round the Mareotic Lake
That the Witch of Atlas knew,
Spoke and set the cocks a-crow.

Swear by those horsemen, by those women
Complexion and form prove superhuman,
That pale, long-visaged company
That air in immortality
Completeness of their passions won;
Now they ride the wintry dawn
When Ben Bulben sets the scene.

Here's the gist of what they mean.

II

Many times man lives and dies
Between his two eternities,
That of race and that of soul,
And ancient Ireland knew it all.
Whether man dies in his bed
Or the rifle knocks him dead,
A brief parting from those dear
Is the worst man has to fear.
Though grave-diggers' toil is long,
Sharp their spades, their muscles strong,
They but thrust their buried men
Back in the human mind again.

III

You that Mitchel's prayer have heard,
'Send war in our time, O Lord!'
Know that when all words are said
And a man is fighting mad,
Something drops from eyes long blind,
He completes his partial mind,
For an instant stands at ease,
Laughs aloud, his heart at peace.
Even the wisest man grows tense
With some sort of violence
Before he can accomplish fate,
Know his work or choose his mate.

IV

Poet and sculptor, do the work,
Nor let the modish painter shirk
What his great forefathers did,
Bring the soul of man to God,
Make him fill the cradles right.

Measurement began our might:
Forms a stark Egyptian thought,
Forms that gentler Phidias wrought.
Michael Angelo left a proof
On the Sistine Chapel roof,
Where but half-awakened Adam
Can disturb globe-trotting Madam
Till her bowels are in heat,
Proof that there's a purpose set
Before the secret working mind:
Profane perfection of mankind.

Quattrocento put in paint
On backgrounds for a God or Saint
Gardens where a soul's at ease;
Where everything that meets the eye,
Flowers and grass and cloudless sky,
Resemble forms that are or seem
When sleepers wake and yet still dream,
And when it's vanished still declare,
With only bed and bedstead there,
That heavens had opened.

                        Gyres run on;
When that greater dream had gone
Calvert and Wilson, Blake and Claude,
Prepared a rest for the people of God,
Palmer's phrase, but after that
Confusion fell upon our thought.

V

Irish poets, learn your trade,
Sing whatever is well made,
Scorn the sort now growing up
All out of shape from toe to top,
Their unremembering hearts and heads
Base-born products of base beds.
Sing the peasantry, and then
Hard-riding country gentlemen,
The holiness of monks, and after
Porter-drinkers' randy laughter;
Sing the lords and ladies gay
That were beaten into the clay
Through seven heroic centuries;
Cast your mind on other days
That we in coming days may be
Still the indomitable Irishry.

VI

Under bare Ben Bulben's head
In Drumcliff churchyard Yeats is laid.
An ancestor was rector there
Long years ago, a church stands near,
By the road an ancient cross.
No marble, no conventional phrase;
On limestone quarried near the spot
By his command these words are cut:

> *Cast a cold eye*
> *On life, on death.*
> *Horseman, pass by!*

Rainer Maria Rilke

Who, if I cried out, would hear me among the
    angels'
hierarchies? and even if one of them pressed me
suddenly against his heart: I would be
    consumed
in that overwhelming existence. For beauty is
    nothing
but the beginning of terror, which we still are
    just able to endure,
and we are so awed because it serenely disdains
to annihilate us. Every angel is terrifying.

"THE FIRST ELEGY," *DUINO ELEGIES*

Rainer Maria Rilke

(Germany, 1875–1926)

Rainer Maria Rilke was born in Prague, into a troubled child-hood. His mother, who had lost a baby girl shortly before Rilke was born, chose to name him René, dress him as a girl, and at times call him "Miss." As her husband's military career stumbled, she felt she had missed out on her aristocratic birthright and did her part to make Rilke believe that his gifts set him apart from his environment. At first Rilke was trained in military schools, in order to have him succeed where his father had not. But he was so unhappy that eventually he was transferred to a gymnasium to prepare for university. Before he left school he completed his first book of poems.

Although he entered Charles University in Prague, Rilke soon left for the cosmopolitan life of Berlin. It was the first of many "elective homelands," as he would call them. He never settled anywhere for long, traveling and living in Russia, France, Sweden, Egypt, Spain, and Switzerland. In 1902 Rilke went to Paris for the first time, to write a monograph on Rodin, and ended up working as Rodin's personal secretary. In the same year, *The Book of Pictures* was published, as Rilke continued to work on its mate, the three parts of *The Book of Hours* (1905). It was under the influence of Paris and the tutelage of Rodin, whose disciplined conception of artistic creation contrasted with Rilke's own notions of inspiration, that his work began to change and evolve; he wrote poems that were eventually collected in two volumes under the title *New Poems* (1907–8). These collections contained his *Ding-Gedichte*, his "thing-poems."

Rilke wrote of his work, "Ah, poems amount to so little when you write them too early in your life. You ought to wait and gather sense and sweetness for a whole lifetime . . . and then, at the very end, you might perhaps be able to write ten good lines. . . . For the sake of a single poem, you must see many cities, many people and Things, you must understand animals, must feel how birds fly, and know the gesture which small flowers make when they open in the morning. . . . You must have memories of many nights of love, each one different from all the others. . . . But you must also have been beside the dying . . . in the room with the open window. . . . And it is not yet enough to have memories. You must be able to forget them when they are many, and you must have immense patience to wait until they return. . . . For the memories themselves are not important. Only when they have changed into our very blood, into glance and gesture . . . only then can it happen that in some very rare hour the first word of a poem arises in their midst and goes forth from them."

In his later work, Rilke began to explore a transformative vision. Setting it up in direct contrast to the notion of the Christian cosmos, he defined an "inner space" where there was no distinction between death and life and everything existed at once. And for Rilke, only poetry was capable of defining, with beauty and in song, this existence.

Rilke's last great work, *The Duino Elegies,* took him ten years to complete. Robert Hass, in his important essay entitled "Looking for Rilke," has written, *"The Duino Elegies* are an argument against our lived, ordinary lives. And it is not surprising that they are. Rilke's special gift as a poet is that he does not seem to speak from the middle of life, that he is always calling us away from it. His poems have the feeling of being written from a great depth in himself. What makes them so seductive is that they also speak to the reader so intimately." The *Elegies,* which Rilke began at the Castle of Duino near Trieste in 1912, were completed, along with *Sonnets to Orpheus,* in February of 1922 at the Château Muzot, in Switzerland.

I am, O Anxious One. Don't you hear my voice
surging forth with all my earthly feelings?
They yearn so high that they have sprouted wings
and whitely fly in circles around your face.
My soul, dressed in silence, rises up
and stands alone before you: can't you see?
Don't you know that my prayer is growing ripe
upon your vision, as upon a tree?

If you are the dreamer, I am what you dream.
But when you want to wake, I am your wish,
and I grow strong with all magnificence
and turn myself into a star's vast silence
above the strange and distant city, Time.

And then that girl the angels came to visit,
she woke also to fruit, frightened by beauty,
given love, shy, in her
so much blossom, the forest
no one had explored, with paths leading everywhere.

They left her alone to walk and to drift
and the spring carried her along.
Her simple and unselfcentered Mary-life
became marvelous and castlelike.
Her life resembled trumpets on the feast days
that reverberated far inside every house;
and she, once so girlish and fragmented,
was so plunged now inside her womb,
and so full inside from that one thing
and so full—enough for a thousand others—
that every creature seemed to throw light on her
and she was like a slope with vines, heavily bearing.

All of you undisturbed cities,
haven't you ever longed for the Enemy?
I'd like to see you besieged by him
for ten endless and ground-shaking years.

Until you were desperate and mad with suffering;
finally in hunger you would feel his weight.
He lies outside the walls like a countryside.
And he knows very well how to endure
longer than the ones he comes to visit.

Climb up on your roofs and look out:
his camp is there, and his morale doesn't falter,
and his numbers do not decrease; he will not grow weaker,
and he sends no one into the city to threaten
or promise, and no one to negotiate.

He is the one who breaks down the walls,
and when he works, he works in silence.

THE WAY IN

Whoever you are; some evening take a step
out of your house, which you know so well.
Enormous space is near, your house lies where it begins,
whoever you are.
Your eyes find it hard to tear themselves
from the sloping threshold, but with your eyes
slowly, slowly, lift one black tree
up, so it stands against the sky: skinny, alone.
With that you have made the world. The world is immense
and like a word that is still growing in the silence.
In the same moment that your will grasps it,
your eyes, feeling its subtlety, will leave it. . . .

ORPHEUS. EURYDICE. HERMES

That was the deep uncanny mine of souls.
Like veins of silver ore, they silently
moved through its massive darkness. Blood welled up
among the roots, on its way to the world of men,
and in the dark it looked as hard as stone.
Nothing else was red.

There were cliffs there,
and forests made of mist. There were bridges
spanning the void, and that great gray blind lake
which hung above its distant bottom
like the sky on a rainy day above a landscape.
And through the gentle, unresisting meadows
one pale path unrolled like a strip of cotton.

Down this path they were coming.

In front, the slender man in the blue cloak—
mute, impatient, looking straight ahead.
In large, greedy, unchewed bites his walk
devoured the path; his hands hung at his sides,
tight and heavy, out of the falling folds,
no longer conscious of the delicate lyre
which had grown into his left arm, like a slip
of roses grafted onto an olive tree.
His senses felt as though they were split in two:
his sight would race ahead of him like a dog,
stop, come back, then rushing off again
would stand, impatient, at the path's next turn,—
but his hearing, like an odor, stayed behind.
Sometimes it seemed to him as though it reached
back to the footsteps of those other two

who were to follow him, up the long path home.
But then, once more, it was just his own steps' echo,
or the wind inside his cloak, that made the sound.
He said to himself, they had to be behind him;
said it aloud and heard it fade away.
They had to be behind him, but their steps
were ominously soft. If only he could
turn around, just once (but looking back
would ruin this entire work, so near
completion), then he could not fail to see them,
those other two, who followed him so softly:

The god of speed and distant messages,
a traveler's hood above his shining eyes,
his slender staff held out in front of him,
and little wings fluttering at his ankles;
and on his left arm, barely touching it: *she.*

A woman so loved that from one lyre there came
more lament than from all lamenting women;
that a whole world of lament arose, in which
all nature reappeared: forest and valley,
road and village, field and stream and animal;
and that around this lament-world, even as
around the other earth, a sun revolved
and a silent star-filled heaven, a lament-
heaven, with its own, disfigured stars—:
So greatly was she loved.

But now she walked beside the graceful god,
her steps constricted by the trailing graveclothes,
uncertain, gentle, and without impatience.
She was deep within herself, like a woman heavy
with child, and did not see the man in front
or the path ascending steeply into life.
Deep within herself. Being dead
filled her beyond fulfillment. Like a fruit
suffused with its own mystery and sweetness,

she was filled with her vast death, which was so new,
she could not understand that it had happened.

She had come into a new virginity
and was untouchable; her sex had closed
like a young flower at nightfall, and her hands
had grown so unused to marriage that the god's
infinitely gentle touch of guidance
hurt her, like an undesired kiss.

She was no longer that woman with blue eyes
who once had echoed through the poet's songs,
no longer the wide couch's scent and island,
and that man's property no longer.

She was already loosened like long hair,
poured out like fallen rain,
shared like a limitless supply.

She was already root.

And when, abruptly,
the god put out his hand to stop her, saying,
with sorrow in his voice: He has turned around—,
she could not understand, and softly answered
Who?

                                    Far away,
dark before the shining exit-gates,
someone or other stood, whose features were
unrecognizable. He stood and saw
how, on the strip of road among the meadows,
with a mournful look, the god of messages
silently turned to follow the small figure
already walking back along the path,
her steps constricted by the trailing graveclothes,
uncertain, gentle, and without impatience.

Archaic Torso of Apollo

We cannot know his legendary head
with eyes like ripening fruit. And yet his torso
is still suffused with brilliance from inside,
like a lamp, in which his gaze, now turned to low,

gleams in all its power. Otherwise
the curved breast could not dazzle you so, nor could
a smile run through the placid hips and thighs
to that dark center where procreation flared.

Otherwise this stone would seem defaced
beneath the translucent cascade of the shoulders
and would not glisten like a wild beast's fur:

would not, from all the borders of itself,
burst like a star: for here there is no place
that does not see you. You must change your life.

Buddha in Glory

Center of all centers, core of cores,
almond self-enclosed and growing sweet—
all this universe, to the furthest stars
and beyond them, is your flesh, your fruit.

Now you feel how nothing clings to you;
your vast shell reaches into endless space,
and there the rich, thick fluids rise and flow.
Illuminated in your infinite peace,

a billion stars go spinning through the night,
blazing high above your head.
But *in* you is the presence that
will be, when all the stars are dead.

Again, Again!

Again, again, even if we know the countryside of love,
and the tiny churchyard with its names mourning,
and the chasm, more and more silent, terrifying, into which the
     others
dropped: we walk out together anyway
beneath the ancient trees, we lie down again,
again, among the flowers, and face the sky.

[For the Sake of a Single Poem]

. . . Ah, poems amount to so little when you write them too early in your life. You ought to wait and gather sense and sweetness for a whole lifetime, and a long one if possible, and then, at the very end, you might perhaps be able to write ten good lines. For poems are not, as people think, simply emotions (one has emotions early enough)—they are experiences. For the sake of a single poem, you must see many cities, many people and Things, you must understand animals, must feel how birds fly, and know the gesture which small flowers make when they open in the morning. You must be able to think back to streets in unknown neighborhoods, to unexpected encounters, and to partings you had long seen coming; to days of childhood whose mystery is still unexplained, to parents whom you had to hurt when they brought in a joy and you didn't pick it up (it was a joy meant for somebody else—); to childhood illnesses that began so strangely with so many profound and difficult transformations, to days in quiet, restrained rooms and to mornings by the sea, to the sea itself, to seas, to nights of travel that rushed along high overhead and went flying with all the stars,—and it is still not enough to be able to think of all that. You must have memories of many nights of love, each one different from all the others, memories of women screaming in labor, and of light, pale, sleeping girls who have just given birth and are closing again. But you must also have been beside the dying, must have sat beside the dead in the room with the open window and the scattered noises. And it is not yet enough to have memories. You must be able to forget them when they are many, and you must have the immense patience to wait until they return. For the memories themselves are not important. Only when they have changed into our very blood, into glance and gesture, and are nameless, no longer to be distinguished from ourselves—only then can it happen that in some very rare hour the first word of a poem arises in their midst and goes forth from them.

CHILDHOOD

Time in school drags along with so much worry,
and waiting, things so dumb and stupid.
Oh loneliness, oh heavy lumpish time . . .
Free at last: lights and colors and noises;
water leaps out of fountains into the air,
and the world is so huge in the woody places.
And moving through it in your short clothes,
and you don't walk the way the others do—
Such marvelous time, such time passing on,
such loneliness.

How strange to see into it all from far away:
men and women, there's a man, one more woman;
children's bright colors make them stand out;
and here a house and now and then a dog
and terror all at once replaced by total trust—
What crazy mourning, what dream, what heaviness,
what deepness without end.

And playing: a hoop, and a bat, and a ball,
in some green place as the light fades away.
And not noticing, you brush against a grownup,
rushing blindly around in tag, half-crazed,
but when the light fades you go with small
puppety steps home, your hand firmly held—
Such oceanic vision that is fading,
such a constant worry, such weight.

Sometimes also kneeling for hours on end
with a tiny sailboat at a grayish pond,
all forgotten because sails more beautiful

than yours go on crossing the circles;
and one had to think always about the pale
narrow face looking up as it sank down—
Oh childhood, what was us going away,
going where? Where?

The Panther

In the Jardin des Plantes, Paris

His vision, from the constantly passing bars,
has grown so weary that it cannot hold
anything else. It seems to him there are
a thousand bars; and behind the bars, no world.

As he paces in cramped circles, over and over,
the movement of his powerful soft strides
is like a ritual dance around a center
in which a mighty will stands paralyzed.

Only at times, the curtain of the pupils
lifts, quietly—. An image enters in,
rushes down through the tensed, arrested muscles,
plunges into the heart and is gone.

Exposed on the cliffs of the heart. Look, how tiny down there,
look: the last village of words and, higher,
(but how tiny) still one last
farmhouse of feeling. Can you see it?
Exposed on the cliffs of the heart. Stoneground
under your hands. Even here, though,
something can bloom; on a silent cliff-edge
an unknowing plant blooms, singing, into the air.
But the one who knows? Ah, he began to know
and is quiet now, exposed on the cliffs of the heart.
While, with their full awareness,
many sure-footed mountain animals pass
or linger. And the great sheltered bird flies, slowly
circling, around the peak's pure denial.—But
without a shelter, here on the cliffs of the heart. . . .

A tree ascended there. Oh pure transcendence!
Oh Orpheus sings! Oh tall tree in the ear!
And all things hushed. Yet even in that silence
a new beginning, beckoning, change appeared.

Creatures of stillness crowded from the bright
unbound forest, out of their lairs and nests;
and it was not from any dullness, not
from fear, that they were so quiet in themselves,

but from simply listening. Bellow, roar, shriek
seemed small inside their hearts. And where there had been
just a makeshift hut to receive the music,

a shelter nailed up out of their darkest longing,
with an entryway that shuddered in the wind—
you built a temple deep inside their hearing.

A god can do it. But will you tell me how
a man can penetrate through the lyre's strings?
Our mind is split. And at the shadowed crossing
of heart-roads, there is no temple for Apollo.

Song, as you have taught it, is not desire,
not wooing any grace that can be achieved;
song is reality. Simple, for a god.
But when can *we* be real? When does he pour

the earth, the stars, into us? Young man,
it is not your loving, even if your mouth
was forced wide open by your own voice—learn

to forget that passionate music. It will end.
True singing is a different breath, about
nothing. A gust inside the god. A wind.

from DUINO ELEGIES

THE FIRST ELEGY

Who, if I cried out, would hear me among the angels'
hierarchies? and even if one of them pressed me
suddenly against his heart: I would be consumed
in that overwhelming existence. For beauty is nothing
but the beginning of terror, which we still are just able to
      endure,
and we are so awed because it serenely disdains
to annihilate us. Every angel is terrifying.
      And so I hold myself back and swallow the call-note
of my dark sobbing. Ah, whom can we ever turn to
in our need? Not angels, not humans,
and already the knowing animals are aware
that we are not really at home in
our interpreted world. Perhaps there remains for us
some tree on a hillside, which every day we can take
into our vision; there remains for us yesterday's street
and the loyalty of a habit so much at ease
when it stayed with us that it moved in and never left.
      Oh and night: there is night, when a wind full of infinite
      space
gnaws at our faces. Whom would it not remain for—that
      longed-after,
mildly disillusioning presence, which the solitary heart
so painfully meets. Is it any less difficult for lovers?
But they keep on using each other to hide their own fate.
      Don't you know *yet*? Fling the emptiness out of your arms
into the spaces we breathe; perhaps the birds
will feel the expanded air with more passionate flying.

Yes—the springtimes needed you. Often a star
was waiting for you to notice it. A wave rolled toward you
out of the distant past, or as you walked
under an open window, a violin
yielded itself to your hearing. All this was mission.
But could you accomplish it? Weren't you always
distracted by expectation, as if every event
announced a beloved? (Where can you find a place
to keep her, with all the huge strange thoughts inside you
going and coming and often staying all night.)
But when you feel longing, sing of women in love;
for their famous passion is still not immortal. Sing
of women abandoned and desolate (you envy them, almost)
who could love so much more purely than those who were
             gratified.
Begin again and again the never-attainable praising;
remember: the hero lives on; even his downfall was
merely a pretext for achieving his final birth.
But Nature, spent and exhausted, takes lovers back
into herself, as if there were not enough strength
to create them a second time. Have you imagined
Gaspara Stampa intensely enough so that any girl
deserted by her beloved might be inspired
by that fierce example of soaring, objectless love
and might say to herself, "Perhaps I can be like her"?
Shouldn't this most ancient of sufferings finally grow
more fruitful for us? Isn't it time that we lovingly
freed ourselves from the beloved and, quivering, endured:
as the arrow endures the bowstring's tension, so that
gathered in the snap of release it can be more than
itself. For there is no place where we can remain.

Voices. Voices. Listen, my heart, as only
saints have listened: until the gigantic call lifted them
off the ground; yet they kept on, impossibly,
kneeling and didn't notice at all:
so complete was their listening. Not that you could endure
God's voice—far from it. But listen to the voice of the wind

and the ceaseless message that forms itself out of silence.
It is murmuring toward you now from those who died young.
Didn't their fate, whenever you stepped into a church
in Naples or Rome, quietly come to address you?
Or high up, some eulogy entrusted you with a mission,
as, last year, on the plaque in Santa Maria Formosa.
What they want of me is that I gently remove the appearance
of injustice about their death—which at times
slightly hinders their souls from proceeding onward.

Of course, it is strange to inhabit the earth no longer,
to give up customs one barely had time to learn,
not to see roses and other promising Things
in terms of a human future; no longer to be
what one was in infinitely anxious hands; to leave
even one's own first name behind, forgetting it
as easily as a child abandons a broken toy.
Strange to no longer desire one's desires. Strange
to see meanings that clung together once, floating away
in every direction. And being dead is hard work
and full of retrieval before one can gradually feel
a trace of eternity.—Though the living are wrong to believe
in the too-sharp distinctions which they themselves have
        created.
Angels (they say) don't know whether it is the living
they are moving among, or the dead. The eternal torrent
whirls all ages along in it, through both realms
forever, and their voices are drowned out in its thunderous
        roar.

In the end, those who were carried off early no longer need us:
they are weaned from earth's sorrows and joys, as gently as
        children
outgrow the soft breasts of their mothers. But we, who do need
such great mysteries, we for whom grief is so often
the source of our spirit's growth—: could we exist without
        them?

Is the legend meaningless that tells how, in the lament for
      Linus,
the daring first notes of song pierced through the barren
      numbness;
and then in the startled space which a youth as lovely as a god
had suddenly left forever, the Void felt for the first time
that harmony which now enraptures and comforts and helps
      us.

THE SECOND ELEGY

Every angel is terrifying. And yet, alas,
I invoke you, almost deadly birds of the soul,
knowing about you. Where are the days of Tobias,
when one of you, veiling his radiance, stood at the front door,
slightly disguised for the journey, no longer appalling;
(a young man like the one who curiously peeked through the
        window).
But if the archangel now, perilous, from behind the stars
took even one step down toward us: our own heart, beating
higher and higher, would beat us to death. Who *are* you?

Early successes, Creation's pampered favorites,
mountain-ranges, peaks growing red in the dawn
of all Beginning,—pollen of the flowering godhead,
joints of pure light, corridors, stairways, thrones,
space formed from essence, shields made of ecstasy, storms
of emotion whirled into rapture, and suddenly, alone:
mirrors, which scoop up the beauty that has streamed from their
        face
and gather it back, into themselves, entire.

But we, when moved by deep feeling, evaporate; we
breathe ourselves out and away; from moment to moment
our emotion grows fainter, like a perfume. Though someone
        may tell us:
"Yes, you've entered my bloodstream, the room, the whole
        springtime
is filled with you . . ."—what does it matter? he can't contain us,
we vanish inside him and around him. And those who are
        beautiful,
oh who can retain them? Appearance ceaselessly rises
in their face, and is gone. Like dew from the morning grass,

what is ours floats into the air, like steam from a dish
of hot food. O smile, where are you going? O upturned glance:
new warm receding wave on the sea of the heart . . .
alas, but that is what we *are*. Does the infinite space
we dissolve into, taste of us then? Do the angels really
reabsorb only the radiance that streamed out from themselves,
      or
sometimes, as if by an oversight, is there a trace
of our essence in it as well? Are we mixed in with their
features even as slightly as that vague look
in the faces of pregnant women? They do not notice it
(how could they notice) in their swirling return to themselves.

Lovers, if they knew how, might utter strange, marvelous
words in the night air. For it seems that everything
hides us. Look: trees do exist; the houses
that we live in still stand. We alone
fly past all things, as fugitive as the wind.
And all things conspire to keep silent about us, half
out of shame perhaps, half as unutterable hope.

Lovers, gratified in each other, I am asking *you*
about us. You hold each other. Where is your proof?
Look, sometimes I find that my hands have become aware
of each other, or that my time-worn face
shelters itself inside them. That gives me a slight
sensation. But who would dare to exist, just for that?
You, though, who in the other's passion
grow until, overwhelmed, he begs you:
"No *more* . . ."; you who beneath his hands
swell with abundance, like autumn grapes;
you who may disappear because the other has wholly
emerged: I am asking *you* about us. I know,
you touch so blissfully because the caress preserves,
because the place you so tenderly cover
does not vanish; because underneath it
you feel pure duration. So you promise eternity, almost,
from the embrace. And yet, when you have survived

the terror of the first glances, the longing at the window,
and the first walk together, once only, through the garden:
lovers, *are* you the same? When you lift yourselves up
to each other's mouth and your lips join, drink against drink:
oh how strangely each drinker seeps away from his action.

Weren't you astonished by the caution of human gestures
on Attic gravestones? Wasn't love and departure
placed so gently on shoulders that it seemed to be made
of a different substance than in our world? Remember the
        hands,
how weightlessly they rest, though there is power in the torsos.
These self-mastered figures know: "We can go this far,
this is ours, to touch one another this lightly; the gods
can press down harder upon us. But that is the gods' affair."

If only we too could discover a pure, contained,
human place, our own strip of fruit-bearing soil
between river and rock. For our own heart always exceeds us,
as theirs did. And we can no longer follow it, gazing
into images that soothe it or into the godlike bodies
where, measured more greatly, it achieves a greater repose.

THE SIXTH ELEGY

Fig-tree, for such a long time I have found meaning
in the way you almost completely omit your blossoms
and urge your pure mystery, unproclaimed,
into the early ripening fruit.
Like the curved pipe of a fountain, your arching boughs drive
            the sap
downward and up again: and almost without awakening
it bursts out of sleep, into its sweetest achievement.
Like the god stepping into the swan.

                     ˙ . . . . . . But *we* still linger, alas,
we, whose pride is in blossoming; we enter the overdue
interior of our final fruit and are already betrayed.
In only a few does the urge to action rise up
so powerfully that they stop, glowing in their heart's
            abundance,
while, like the soft night air, the temptation to blossom
touches their tender mouths, touches their eyelids, softly:
heroes perhaps, and those chosen to disappear early,
whose veins Death the gardener twists into a different pattern.
These plunge on ahead: in advance of their own smile
like the team of galloping horses before the triumphant
pharaoh in the mildly hollowed reliefs at Karnak.

The hero is strangely close to those who died young.
            Permanence
does not concern him. He lives in continual ascent,
moving on into the ever-changed constellation
of perpetual danger. Few could find him there. But
Fate, which is silent about us, suddenly grows inspired
and sings him into the storm of his onrushing world.
I hear no one like *him.* All at once I am pierced
by his darkened voice, carried on the streaming air.

Then how gladly I would hide from the longing to be once
        again
oh a boy once again, with my life before me, to sit
leaning on future arms and reading of Samson,
how from his mother first nothing, then everything, was born.

Wasn't he a hero inside you, mother? didn't
his imperious choosing already begin there, in you?
Thousands seethed in your womb, wanting to be *him*,
but look: he grasped and excluded—, chose and prevailed.
And if he demolished pillars, it was when he burst
from the world of your body into the narrower world, where
        again
he chose and prevailed. O mothers of heroes, O sources
of ravaging floods! You ravines into which
virgins have plunged, lamenting,
from the highest rim of the heart, sacrifices to the son.
    For whenever the hero stormed through the stations of
        love,
each heartbeat intended for him lifted him up, beyond it;
and, turning away, he stood there, at the end of all
        smiles,—transfigured.

THE NINTH ELEGY

Why, if this interval of being can be spent serenely
in the form of a laurel, slightly darker than all
other green, with tiny waves on the edges
of every leaf (like the smile of a breeze)—: why then
have to be human—and, escaping from fate,
keep longing for fate? . . .
                     Oh *not* because happiness *exists*,
that too-hasty profit snatched from approaching loss.
Not out of curiosity, not as practice for the heart, which
would exist in the laurel too. . . .

But because *truly* being here is so much; because everything
      here
apparently needs us, this fleeting world, which in some strange
      way
keeps calling to us. Us, the most fleeting of all.
Once for each thing. Just once; no more. And we too,
just once. And never again. But to have been
this once, completely, even if only once:
to have been at one with the earth, seems beyond undoing.

And so we keep pressing on, trying to achieve it,
trying to hold it firmly in our simple hands,
in our overcrowded gaze, in our speechless heart.
Trying to become it.—Whom can we give it to? We would
hold on to it all, forever . . . Ah, but what can we take along
into that other realm? Not the art of looking,
which is learned so slowly, and nothing that happened here.
      Nothing.
The sufferings, then. And, above all, the heaviness,
and the long experience of love,—just what is wholly

unsayable. But later, among the stars,
what good is it—*they* are *better* as they are: unsayable.
For when the traveler returns from the mountain-slopes into the
      valley,
he brings, not a handful of earth, unsayable to others, but
      instead
some word he has gained, some pure word, the yellow and blue
gentian. Perhaps we are *here* in order to say: house,
bridge, fountain, gate, pitcher, fruit-tree, window—
at most: column, tower. . . . But to *say* them, you must
      understand,
oh to say them *more* intensely than the Things themselves
ever dreamed of existing. Isn't the secret intent
of this taciturn earth, when it forces lovers together,
that inside their boundless emotion all things may shudder
      with joy?
Threshold: what it means for two lovers
to be wearing down, imperceptibly, the ancient threshold of
      their door—
they too, after the many who came before them
and before those to come. . . . , lightly.

Here is the time for the *sayable, here* is its homeland.
Speak and bear witness. More than ever
the Things that we might experience are vanishing, for
what crowds them out and replaces them is an imageless act.
An act under a shell, which easily cracks open as soon as
the business inside outgrows it and seeks new limits.
Between the hammers our heart
endures, just as the tongue does
between the teeth and, despite that,
still is able to praise.

Praise this world to the angel, not the unsayable one,
you can't impress *him* with glorious emotion; in the universe
where he feels more powerfully, you are a novice. So show him
something simple which, formed over generations,
lives as our own, near our hand and within our gaze.

Tell him of Things. He will stand astonished; as *you* stood
by the rope-maker in Rome or the potter along the Nile.
Show him how happy a Thing can be, how innocent and ours,
how even lamenting grief purely decides to take form,
serves as a Thing, or dies into a Thing—, and blissfully
escapes far beyond the violin.—And these Things,
which live by perishing, know you are praising them; transient,
they look to us for deliverance: us, the most transient of all.
They want us to change them, utterly, in our invisible heart,
within—oh endlessly—within us! Whoever we may be at last.

Earth, isn't this what you want: to arise within us,
invisible? Isn't it your dream
to be wholly invisible someday?—O Earth: invisible!
What, if not transformation, is your urgent command?
Earth, my dearest, I will. Oh believe me, you no longer
need your springtimes to win me over—one of them,
ah, even one, is already too much for my blood.
Unspeakably I have belonged to you, from the first.
You were always right, and your holiest inspiration
is our intimate companion, Death.

Look, I am living. On what? Neither childhood nor future
grows any smaller . . . . . Superabundant being
wells up in my heart.

The Tenth Elegy

Someday, emerging at last from the violent insight,
let me sing our jubilation and praise to assenting angels.
Let not even one of the clearly-struck hammers of my heart
fail to sound because of a slack, a doubtful,
or a broken string. Let my joyfully streaming face
make me more radiant; let my hidden weeping arise
and blossom. How dear you will be to me then, you nights
of anguish. Why didn't I kneel more deeply to accept you,
inconsolable sisters, and, surrendering, lose myself
in your loosened hair. How we squander our hours of pain.
How we gaze beyond them into the bitter duration
to see if they have an end. Though they are really
our winter-enduring foliage, our dark evergreen,
one season in our inner year—, not only a season
in time—, but are place and settlement, foundation and soil and
　　　　home.

But how alien, alas, are the streets of the city of grief,
where, in the false silence formed of continual uproar,
the figure cast from the mold of emptiness stoutly
swaggers: the gilded noise, the bursting memorial.
Oh how completely an angel would stamp out their market of
　　　　solace,
bounded by the church with its ready-made consolations:
clean and disenchanted and shut as a post-office on Sunday.
Farther out, though, the city's edges are curling with carnival.
Swings of freedom! Divers and jugglers of zeal!
And the shooting-gallery's targets of prettified happiness,
which jump and kick back with a tinny sound
when hit by some better marksman. From cheers to chance
he goes staggering on, as booths with all sorts of attractions
are wooing, drumming, and bawling. For adults only

there is something special to see: how money multiplies, naked,
right there on stage, money's genitals, nothing concealed,
the whole action—, educational, and guaranteed
to increase your potency . . . .
. . . . Oh, but a little farther,
beyond the last of the billboards, plastered with signs for
        "Deathless,"
that bitter beer which seems so sweet to its drinkers
as long as they chew fresh distractions in between sips . . . ,
just in back of the billboard, just behind, the view becomes *real*.
Children are playing, and lovers are holding hands, to the side,
solemnly in the meager grass, and dogs are doing what is
        natural.
The young man is drawn on, farther; perhaps he is in love with
        a young
Lament . . . . . He comes out behind her, into the meadows. She
        says:
—It's a long walk. We live way out there . . . .
                                        Where? And the youth
follows. He is touched by her manner. Her shoulders, her
        neck—, perhaps
she is of noble descent. But he leaves her, turns around,
looks back, waves . . . What's the use? She is a Lament.

Only those who died young, in their first condition
of timeless equanimity, while they are being weaned,
follow her lovingly. She waits
for girls and befriends them. Shows them, gently,
what she is wearing. Pearls of grief and the fine-spun
veils of patience.—With young men she walks
in silence.

But there, in the valley, where they live, one of the elder
        Laments
answers the youth when he questions her:—Long ago,
she says, we Laments were a powerful race. Our forefathers
        worked
the mines, up there in the mountain-range; sometimes even

among men you can find a polished nugget of primal grief
or a chunk of petrified rage from the slag of an ancient volcano.
Yes, that came from up there. We used to be rich.—

And gently she guides him through the vast landscape of
        Lament,
shows him the pillars of the temples, and the ruined walls
of those castles from which, long ago, the princes of Lament
wisely ruled the land. Shows him the tall
trees of tears and the fields of blossoming grief
(the living know it just as a mild green shrub);
shows him the herds of sorrow, grazing,—and sometimes
a startled bird, flying low through their upward gaze,
far away traces the image of its solitary cry.—
In the twilight she leads him out to the graves of the elders
who gave warning to the race of Laments, the sibyls and
        prophets.
But as night approaches, they move more softly, and soon
the sepulchre rises up
like a moon, watching over everything. Brother to the one on
        the Nile,
the lofty Sphinx—: the taciturn chamber's
countenance.
And they look in wonder at the regal head that has silently
lifted the human face
to the scale of the stars, forever.

Still dizzy from recent death, his sight
cannot grasp it. But her gaze
frightens an owl from behind the rim of the crown. And the
        bird,
with slow downstrokes, brushes along the cheek,
the one with the fuller curve,
and faintly, in the dead youth's new
sense of hearing, as upon a double
unfolded page, it sketches the indescribable outline.

And higher, the stars. The new stars of the land of grief.
Slowly the Lament names them:—Look, there:

the *Rider*, the *Staff*, and the larger constellation
called *Garland of Fruit*. Then, farther up toward the Pole:
Cradle; Path; The Burning Book; Puppet; Window.
But there, in the southern sky, pure as the lines
on the palm of a blessed hand, the clear sparkling *M*
that stands for Mothers . . . . . . —

But the dead youth must go on by himself, and silently the
        elder Lament
takes him as far as the ravine,
where shimmering in the moonlight
is the fountainhead of joy. With reverence
she names it and says:—Among men
it is a mighty stream.—

They stand at the foot of the mountain-range.
And she embraces him, weeping.

Alone, he climbs on, up the mountains of primal grief.
And not once do his footsteps echo from the soundless path.

                                    *

But if the endlessly dead awakened a symbol in us,
perhaps they would point to the catkins hanging from the bare
branches of the hazel-trees, or
would evoke the raindrops that fall onto the dark earth in
        springtime.—

And we, who have always thought
of happiness as *rising*, would feel
the emotion that almost overwhelms us
whenever a happy thing *falls*.

HART CRANE

So to thine Everpresence, beyond time,
Like spears ensanguined of one tolling star
That bleeds infinity—the orphic strings,
Sidereal phalanxes, leap and converge:
—One Song, one Bridge of Fire! Is it Cathay,
Now pity steeps the grass and rainbows ring
The serpent with the eagle in the leaves . . . ?
Whispers antiphonal in azure swing.

"Atlantis," *THE BRIDGE*

Hart Crane

(United States, 1899–1932)

Hart Crane was a native of Ohio, born in the last July of the nineteenth century of solid American stock. His father, Clarence Arthur Crane, was a successful candy manufacturer in Cleveland. Crane, who was a serious and avid student of literature, history, and aesthetics throughout his life, began his passionate reading as a youth. When he was thirteen he started writing poetry. At seventeen he and his mother moved to his grandfather's fruit ranch on Isle of Pines, near Cuba, but he soon returned, with a short stop in New York, to Cleveland, where he worked in a munitions plant and a shipyard during World War I.

In 1924 he returned to New York, where he pursued life as a writer and occasionally worked for magazines and advertising agencies. Often thought of as a city poet, he in fact retained the visual memory of the landscapes of his Ohio childhood, as well as of broader rural travels, and his poetry offers as much natural as urban imagery. In 1926 he published his first collection of poems, *White Buildings*. For his masterpiece, *The Bridge*, published in 1930, Crane used T. S. Eliot's *The Waste Land* as a structural model. Thematically, however, Crane wished to offer an alternative to what he considered the cultural pessimism of Eliot's poem. Crane referred to *The Bridge* as "a mystical synthesis of America." Malcolm Cowley called it "the most important volume of American poetry since Whitman's *Leaves of Grass*."

Although today Crane is considered one of the most important American poets of the twentieth century, during his lifetime and immediately after, he suffered at the hands of the critics who seemed to miss the point of his most inspired work. Crane's vision of America was big, Whitmanesque in its wish to "embrace the multitudes." He saw the things of this world caught in that moment when they would rise beyond themselves and the universe of the corporeal. In this he was a brother to Rimbaud and his elaborate transformation of the commonplace sensory realm—as Crane, in turn, would seem a spiritual brother to the young Allen Ginsberg. Crane wrote to Harriet Monroe that he wished to locate and articulate a logic of metaphor—or, as he himself put it, "In poetry the *rationale* of metaphor belongs to another order of experience than science, and is not to be limited by a scientific and arbitrary code of relationships either in verbal inflections or concepts."

Despite his heroic and optimistic vision, Crane was often personally troubled. Beginning in his childhood, his mother was excessively dependent on him emotionally. After she and Crane's father divorced, she came to New York with her own mother and moved into her son's one-bedroom apartment, prevailing on him for attention. Nor did Crane get along well with his father, upon whom he often depended for financial support. It was a complicated web of interdependence that never entirely left him free for his own emotional life. Being in New York began to compound Crane's sense of his personal difficulties, and increasingly he left the city whenever he could afford to. He traveled to New England and Europe, but ultimately despaired of his ability to continue writing. At the age of thirty-two, coming back from Mexico aboard the *Orizaba*, about 300 miles from Cuba, he walked to the back of the boat, removed the coat he was wearing, and released himself to the water.

REPOSE OF RIVERS

The willows carried a slow sound,
A sarabande the wind mowed on the mead.
I could never remember
That seething, steady leveling of the marshes
Till age had brought me to the sea.

Flags, weeds. And remembrance of steep alcoves
Where cypresses shared the noon's
Tyranny; they drew me into hades almost.
And mammoth turtles climbing sulphur dreams
Yielded, while sun-silt rippled them
Asunder . . .

How much I would have bartered! the black gorge
And all the singular nestings in the hills
Where beavers learn stitch and tooth.
The pond I entered once and quickly fled—
I remember now its singing willow rim.

And finally, in that memory all things nurse;
After the city that I finally passed
With scalding unguents spread and smoking darts
The monsoon cut across the delta
At gulf gates . . . There, beyond the dykes

I heard wind flaking sapphire, like this summer,
And willows could not hold more steady sound.

LACHRYMAE CHRISTI

Whitely, while benzine
Rinsings from the moon
Dissolve all but the windows of the mills
(Inside the sure machinery
Is still
And curdled only where a sill
Sluices its one unyielding smile)

Immaculate venom binds
The fox's teeth, and swart
Thorns freshen on the year's
First blood. From flanks unfended,
Twanged red perfidies of spring
Are trillion on the hill.

And the nights opening
Chant pyramids,—
Anoint with innocence,—recall
To music and retrieve what perjuries
Had galvanized the eyes.

        While chime
Beneath and all around
Distilling clemencies,—worms'
Inaudible whistle, tunneling
Not penitence
But song, as these
Perpetual fountains, vines,—

Thy Nazarene and tinder eyes.
(Let sphinxes from the ripe

Borage of death have cleared my tongue
Once and again; vermin and rod
No longer bind. Some sentient cloud
Of tears flocks through the tendoned loam:
Betrayed stones slowly speak.)

Names peeling from Thine eyes
And their undimming lattices of flame,
Spell out in palm and pain
Compulsion of the year, O Nazarene.

Lean long from sable, slender boughs,
Unstanched and luminous. And as the nights
Strike from Thee perfect spheres,
Lift up in lilac-emerald breath the grail
Of earth again—
                    Thy face
From charred and riven stakes, O
Dionysus, Thy
Unmangled target smile.

PASSAGE

Where the cedar leaf divides the sky
I heard the sea.
In sapphire arenas of the hills
I was promised an improved infancy.

Sulking, sanctioning the sun,
My memory I left in a ravine,—
Casual louse that tissues the buckwheat,
Aprons rocks, congregates pears
In moonlit bushels
And wakens alleys with a hidden cough.

Dangerously the summer burned
(I had joined the entrainments of the wind).
The shadows of boulders lengthened my back:
In the bronze gongs of my cheeks
The rain dried without odour.

"It is not long, it is not long;
See where the red and black
Vine-stanchioned valleys—": but the wind
Died speaking through the ages that you know
And hug, chimney-sooted heart of man!
So was I turned about and back, much as your smoke
Compiles a too well-known biography.

The evening was a spear in the ravine
That throve through very oak. And had I walked
The dozen particular decimals of time?
Touching an opening laurel, I found
A thief beneath, my stolen book in hand.

"Why are you back here—smiling an iron coffin?"
"To argue with the laurel," I replied:
"Am justified in transience, fleeing
Under the constant wonder of your eyes—."

He closed the book. And from the Ptolemies
Sand troughed us in a glittering abyss.
A serpent swam a vertex to the sun
—On unpaced beaches leaned its tongue and drummed.
What fountains did I hear? what icy speeches?
Memory, committed to the page, had broke.

RECITATIVE

Regard the capture here, O Janus-faced,
As double as the hands that twist this glass.
Such eyes at search or rest you cannot see;
Reciting pain or glee, how can you bear!

Twin shadowed halves: the breaking second holds
In each the skin alone, and so it is
I crust a plate of vibrant mercury
Borne cleft to you, and brother in the half.

Inquire this much-exacting fragment smile,
Its drums and darkest blowing leaves ignore,—
Defer though, revocation of the tears
That yield attendance to one crucial sign.

Look steadily—how the wind feasts and spins
The brain's disk shivered against lust. Then watch
While darkness, like an ape's face, falls away,
And gradually white buildings answer day.

Let the same nameless gulf beleaguer us—
Alike suspend us from atrocious sums
Built floor by floor on shafts of steel that grant
The plummet heart, like Absalom, no stream.

The highest tower,—let her ribs palisade
Wrenched gold of Nineveh;—yet leave the tower.
The bridge swings over salvage, beyond wharves;
A wind abides the ensign of your will . . .

In alternating bells have you not heard
All hours clapped dense into a single stride?
Forgive me for an echo of these things,
And let us walk through time with equal pride.

For the Marriage of Faustus and Helen

> "And so we may arrive by Talmud skill
> And profane Greek to raise the building up
> Of Helen's house against the Ismaelite,
> King of Thogarma, and his habergeons
> Brimstony, blue and fiery; and the force
> Of King Abaddon, and the beast of Cittim;
> Which Rabbi David Kimchi, Onkelos,
> And Aben Ezra do interpret Rome."
>
> THE ALCHEMIST

I

The mind has shown itself at times
Too much the baked and labeled dough
Divided by accepted multitudes.
Across the stacked partitions of the day—
Across the memoranda, baseball scores,
The stenographic smiles and stock quotations
Smutty wings flash out equivocations.

The mind is brushed by sparrow wings;
Numbers, rebuffed by asphalt, crowd
The margins of the day, accent the curbs,
Convoying divers dawns on every corner
To druggist, barber and tobacconist,
Until the graduate opacities of evening
Take them away as suddenly to somewhere
Virginal perhaps, less fragmentary, cool.

*There is the world dimensional for
those untwisted by the love of things
irreconcilable . . .*

And yet, suppose some evening I forgot
The fare and transfer, yet got by that way
Without recall,—lost yet poised in traffic.
Then I might find your eyes across an aisle,
Still flickering with those prefigurations—
Prodigal, yet uncontested now,
Half-riant before the jerky window frame.

There is some way, I think, to touch
Those hands of yours that count the nights
Stippled with pink and green advertisements.
And now, before its arteries turn dark
I would have you meet this bartered blood.
Imminent in his dream, none better knows
The white wafer cheek of love, or offers words
Lightly as moonlight on the eaves meets snow.

Reflective conversion of all things
At your deep blush, when ecstasies thread
The limbs and belly, when rainbows spread
Impinging on the throat and sides . . .
Inevitable, the body of the world
Weeps in inventive dust for the hiatus
That winks above it, bluet in your breasts.

The earth may glide diaphanous to death;
But if I lift my arms it is to bend
To you who turned away once, Helen, knowing
The press of troubled hands, too alternate
with steel and soil to hold you endlessly.
I meet you, therefore, in that eventual flame
You found in final chains, no captive then—
Beyond their million brittle, bloodshot eyes;
White, through white cities passed on to assume
That world which comes to each of us alone.

Accept a lone eye riveted to your plane,
Bent axle of devotion along companion ways

That beat, continuous, to hourless days—
One inconspicuous, glowing orb of praise.

II

Brazen hynotics glitter here;
Glee shifts from foot to foot,
Magnetic to their tremolo.
This crashing opéra bouffe,
Blest excursion! this ricochet
From roof to roof—
Know, Olympians, we are breathless
While nigger cupids scour the stars!

A thousand light shrugs balance us
Through snarling hails of melody.
White shadows slip across the floor
Splayed like cards from a loose hand;
Rhythmic ellipses lead into canters
Until somewhere a rooster banters.

Greet naïvely—yet intrepidly
New soothings, new amazements
That cornets introduce at every turn—
And you may fall downstairs with me
With perfect grace and equanimity.
Or, plaintively scud past shores
Where, by strange harmonic laws
All relatives, serene and cool,
Sit rocked in patent armchairs.

O, I have known metallic paradises
Where cuckoos clucked to finches
Above the deft catastrophes of drums.
While titters hailed the groans of death
Beneath gyrating awnings I have seen
The incunabula of the divine grotesque.
This music has a reassuring way.

The siren of the springs of guilty song—
Let us take her on the incandescent wax
Striated with nuances, nervosities
That we are heir to: she is still so young,
We cannot frown upon her as she smiles,
Dipping here in this cultivated storm
Among slim skaters of the gardened skies.

III

Capped arbiter of beauty in this street
That narrows darkly into motor dawn,—
You, here beside me, delicate ambassador
Of intricate slain numbers that arise
In whispers, naked of steel;
                                    religious gunman!
Who faithfully, yourself, will fall too soon,
And in other ways than as the wind settles
On the sixteen thrifty bridges of the city:
Let us unbind our throats of fear and pity.

                                    We even,
Who drove speediest destruction
In corymbulous formations of mechanics,—
Who hurried the hill breezes, spouting malice
Plangent over meadows, and looked down
On rifts of torn and empty houses
Like old women with teeth unjubilant
That waited faintly, briefly and in vain:

We know, eternal gunman, our flesh remembers
The tensile boughs, the nimble blue plateaus,
The mounted, yielding cities of the air!

That saddled sky that shook down vertical
Repeated play of fire—no hypogeum
Of wave or rock was good against one hour.

We did not ask for that, but have survived,
And will persist to speak again before
All stubble streets that have not curved
To memory, or known the ominous lifted arm
That lowers down the arc of Helen's brow
To saturate with blessing and dismay.

A goose, tobacco and cologne—
Three-winged and gold-shod prophecies of heaven,
The lavish heart shall always have to leaven
And spread with bells and voices, and atone
The abating shadows of our conscript dust.

Anchises' navel, dripping of the sea,—
The hands Erasmus dipped in gleaming tides,
Gathered the voltage of blown blood and vine;
Delve upward for the new and scattered wine,
O brother-thief of time, that we recall.
Laugh out the meager penance of their days
Who dare not share with us the breath released,
The substance drilled and spent beyond repair
For golden, or the shadow of gold hair.

Distinctly praise the years, whose volatile
Blamed bleeding hands extend and thresh the height
The imagination spans beyond despair,
Outpacing bargain, vocable and prayer.

O Carib Isle!

The tarantula rattling at the lily's foot
Across the feet of the dead, laid in white sand
Near the coral beach—nor zigzag fiddle crabs
Side-stilting from the path (that shift, subvert
And anagrammatize your name)—No, nothing here
Below the palsy that one eucalyptus lifts
In wrinkled shadows—mourns.

                              And yet suppose
I count these nacreous frames of tropic death,
Brutal necklaces of shells around each grave
Squared off so carefully. Then

To the white sand I may speak a name, fertile
Albeit in a stranger tongue. Tree names, flower names
Deliberate, gainsay death's brittle crypt. Meanwhile
The wind that knots itself in one great death—
Coils and withdraws. So syllables want breath.

But where is the Captain of this doubloon isle
Without a turnstile? Who but catchword crabs
Patrols the dry groins of the underbrush?
What man, or What
Is Commissioner of mildew throughout the ambushed senses?
His Carib mathematics web the eyes' baked lenses!

Under the poinciana, of a noon or afternoon
Let fiery blossoms clot the light, render my ghost
Sieved upward, white and black along the air
Until it meets the blue's comedian host.

Let not the pilgrim see himself again
For slow evisceration bound like those huge terrapin
Each daybreak on the wharf, their brine-caked eyes;
—Spiked, overturned; such thunder in their strain!
And clenched beaks coughing for the surge again!

Slagged of the hurricane—I, cast within its flow,
Congeal by afternoons here, satin and vacant.
You have given me the shell, Satan,—carbonic amulet
Sere of the sun exploded in the sea.

Voyages

I

Above the fresh ruffles of the surf
Bright striped urchins flay each other with sand.
They have contrived a conquest for shell shucks,
And their fingers crumble fragments of baked weed
Gaily digging and scattering.

And in answer to their treble interjections
The sun beats lightning on the waves,
The waves fold thunder on the sand;
And could they hear me I would tell them:

O brilliant kids, frisk with your dog,
Fondle your shells and sticks, bleached
By time and the elements; but there is a line
You must not cross nor ever trust beyond it
Spry cordage of your bodies to caresses
Too lichen-faithful from too wide a breast.
The bottom of the sea is cruel.

II

—And yet this great wink of eternity,
Of rimless floods, unfettered leewardings,
Samite sheeted and processioned where
Her undinal vast belly moonward bends,
Laughing the wrapt inflections of our love;

Take this Sea, whose diapason knells
On scrolls of silver snowy sentences,
The sceptred terror of whose sessions rends

As her demeanors motion well or ill,
All but the pieties of lovers' hands.

And onward, as bells off San Salvador
Salute the crocus lustres of the stars,
In these poinsettia meadows of her tides,—
Adagios of islands, O my Prodigal,
Complete the dark confessions her veins spell.

Mark how her turning shoulders wind the hours,
And hasten while her penniless rich palms
Pass superscription of bent foam and wave,—
Hasten, while they are true,—sleep, death, desire,
Close round one instant in one floating flower.

Bind us in time, O Seasons clear, and awe.
O minstrel galleons of Carib fire,
Bequeath us to no earthly shore until
Is answered in the vortex of our grave
The seal's wide spindrift gaze toward paradise.

III

Infinite consanguinity it bears—
This tendered theme of you that light
Retrieves from sea plains where the sky
Resigns a breast that every wave enthrones;
While ribboned water lanes I wind
Are laved and scattered with no stroke
Wide from your side, whereto this hour
The sea lifts, also, reliquary hands.

And so, admitted through black swollen gates
That must arrest all distance otherwise,—
Past whirling pillars and lithe pediments,
Light wrestling there incessantly with light,
Star kissing star through wave on wave unto
Your body rocking!
                              and where death, if shed,

Presumes no carnage, but this single change,—
Upon the steep floor flung from dawn to dawn
The silken skilled transmemberment of song;

Permit me voyage, love, into your hands . . .

IV

Whose counted smile of hours and days, suppose
I know as spectrum of the sea and pledge
Vastly now parting gulf on gulf of wings
Whose circles bridge, I know, (from palms to the severe
Chilled albatross's white immutability)
No stream of greater love advancing now
Than, singing, this mortality alone
Through clay aflow immortally to you.

All fragrance irrefragibly, and claim
Madly meeting logically in this hour
And region that is ours to wreathe again,
Portending eyes and lips and making told
The chancel port and portion of our June—

Shall they not stem and close in our own steps
Bright staves of flowers and quills to-day as I
Must first be lost in fatal tides to tell?

In signature of the incarnate word
The harbor shoulders to resign in mingling
Mutual blood, transpiring as foreknown
And widening noon within your breast for gathering
All bright insinuations that my years have caught
For islands where must lead inviolably
Blue latitudes and levels of your eyes,—

In this expectant, still exclaim receive
The secret oar and petals of all love.

V

Meticulous, past midnight in clear rime,
Infrangible and lonely, smooth as though cast
Together in one merciless white blade—
The bay estuaries fleck the hard sky limits.

—As if too brittle or too clear to touch!
The cables of our sleep so swiftly filed,
Already hang, shred ends from remembered stars.
One frozen trackless smile . . . What words
Can strangle this deaf moonlight? For we

Are overtaken. Now no cry, no sword
Can fasten or deflect this tidal wedge,
Slow tyranny of moonlight, moonlight loved
And changed . . . "There's

Nothing like this in the world," you say,
Knowing I cannot touch your hand and look
Too, into that godless cleft of sky
Where nothing turns but dead sands flashing.

"—And never to quite understand!" No,
In all the argosy of your bright hair I dreamed
Nothing so flagless as this piracy.

                        But now
Draw in your head, alone and too tall here.
Your eyes already in the slant of drifting foam;
Your breath sealed by the ghosts I do not know:
Draw in your head and sleep the long way home.

VI

Where icy and bright dungeons lift
Of swimmers their lost morning eyes,
And ocean rivers, churning, shift
Green borders under stranger skies,

Steadily as a shell secretes
Its beating leagues of monotone,
Or as many waters trough the sun's
Red kelson past the cape's wet stone;

O rivers mingling toward the sky
And harbor of the phoenix' breast—
My eyes pressed black against the prow,
—Thy derelict and blinded guest

Waiting, afire, what name, unspoke,
I cannot claim: let thy waves rear
More savage than the death of kings,
Some splintered garland for the seer.

Beyond siroccos harvesting
The solstice thunders, crept away,
Like a cliff swinging or a sail
Flung into April's inmost day—

Creation's blithe and petalled word
To the lounged goddess when she rose
Conceding dialogue with eyes
That smile unsearchable repose—

Still fervid covenant, Belle Isle,
—Unfolded floating dais before

Which rainbows twine continual hair—
Belle Isle, white echo of the oar!

The imaged Word, it is, that holds
Hushed willows anchored in its glow.
It is the unbetrayable reply
Whose accent no farewell can know.

THE BROKEN TOWER

The bell-rope that gathers God at dawn
Dispatches me as though I dropped down the knell
Of a spent day—to wander the cathedral lawn
From pit to crucifix, feet chill on steps from hell.

Have you not heard, have you not seen that corps
Of shadows in the tower, whose shoulders sway
Antiphonal carillons launched before
The stars are caught and hived in the sun's ray?

The bells, I say, the bells break down their tower;
And swing I know not where. Their tongues engrave
Membrane through marrow, my long-scattered score
Of broken intervals . . . And I, their sexton slave!

Oval encyclicals in canyons heaping
The impasse high with choir. Banked voices slain!
Pagodas, campaniles with reveilles outleaping—
O terraced echoes prostrate on the plain! . . .

And so it was I entered the broken world
To trace the visionary company of love, its voice
An instant in the wind (I know not whither hurled)
But not for long to hold each desperate choice.

My word I poured. But was it cognate, scored
Of that tribunal monarch of the air
Whose thigh embronzes earth, strikes crystal Word
In wounds pledged once to hope—cleft to despair?

The steep encroachments of my blood left me
No answer (could blood hold such a lofty tower

As flings the question true?)—or is it she
Whose sweet mortality stirs latent power?—

And through whose pulse I hear, counting the strokes
My veins recall and add, revived and sure
The angelus of wars my chest evokes:
What I hold healed, original now, and pure . . .

And builds, within, a tower that is not stone
(Not stone can jacket heaven)—but slip
Of pebbles,—visible wings of silence sown
In azure circles, widening as they dip

The matrix of the heart, lift down the eye
That shrines the quiet lake and swells a tower . . .
The commodious, tall decorum of that sky
Unseals her earth, and lifts love in its shower.

from THE BRIDGE

To Brooklyn Bridge

How many dawns, chill from his rippling rest
The seagull's wings shall dip and pivot him,
Shedding white rings of tumult, building high
Over the chained bay waters Liberty—

Then, with inviolate curve, forsake our eyes
As apparitional as sails that cross
Some page of figures to be filed away;
—Till elevators drop us from our day . . .

I think of cinemas, panoramic sleights
With multitudes bent toward some flashing scene
Never disclosed, but hastened to again,
Foretold to other eyes on the same screen;

And Thee, across the harbor, silver-paced
As though the sun took step of thee, yet left
Some motion ever unspent in thy stride,—
Implicitly thy freedom staying thee!

Out of some subway scuttle, cell or loft
A bedlamite speeds to thy parapets,
Tilting there momently, shrill shirt ballooning,
A jest falls from the speechless caravan.

Down Wall, from girder into street noon leaks,
A rip-tooth of the sky's acetylene;

All afternoon the cloud-flown derricks turn . . .
Thy cables breathe the North Atlantic still.

And obscure as that heaven of the Jews,
Thy guerdon . . . Accolade thou dost bestow
Of anonymity time cannot raise:
Vibrant reprieve and pardon thou dost show.

O harp and altar, of the fury fused,
(How could mere toil align thy choiring strings!)
Terrific threshold of the prophet's pledge,
Prayer of pariah, and the lover's cry,—

Again the traffic lights that skim thy swift
Unfractioned idiom, immaculate sigh of stars,
Beading thy path—condense eternity:
And we have seen night lifted in thine arms.

Under thy shadow by the piers I waited;
Only in darkness is thy shadow clear.
The City's fiery parcels all undone,
Already snow submerges an iron year . . .

O Sleepless as the river under thee,
Vaulting the sea, the prairies' dreaming sod,
Unto us lowliest sometime sweep, descend
And of the curveship lend a myth to God.

Ave Maria

Venient annis, sœcula seris,
Quibus Oceanus vincula rerum
Laxet et ingens pateat tellus
Tiphysque novos detegat orbes
Nec sit terris ultima Thule.

SENECA

Be with me, Luis de San Angel, now—
Witness before the tides can wrest away
The word I bring, O you who reined my suit
Into the Queen's great heart that doubtful day;
For I have seen now what no perjured breath
Of clown nor sage can riddle or gainsay;—
To you, too, Juan Perez, whose counsel fear
And greed adjourned,—I bring you back Cathay!

Columbus alone, gazing toward Spain, invokes the presence of two faithful partisans of his quest . . .

Here waves climb into dusk on gleaming mail;
Invisible valves of the sea,—locks, tendons
Crested and creeping, troughing corridors
That fall back yawning to another plunge.
Slowly the sun's red caravel drops light
Once more behind us. . . . It is morning there—
O where our Indian emperies lie revealed,
Yet lost, all, let this keel one instant yield!

I thought of Genoa; and this truth, now proved,
That made me exile in her streets, stood me
More absolute than ever—biding the moon
Till dawn should clear that dim frontier, first seen

—The Chan's great continent. . . . Then faith, not fear
Nigh surged me witless. . . . Hearing the surf near—
I, wonder-breathing, kept the watch,—saw
The first palm chevron the first lighted hill.

And lowered. And they came out to us crying,
"The Great White Birds!" (O Madre María, still
One ship of these thou grantest safe returning;
Assure us through thy mantle's ageless blue!)
And record of more, floating in a casque,
Was tumbled from us under bare poles scudding;
And later hurricanes may claim more pawn. . . .
For here between two worlds, another, harsh,

This third, of water, tests the word; lo, here
Bewilderment and mutiny heap whelming
Laughter, and shadow cuts sleep from the heart
Almost as though the Moor's flung scimitar
Found more than flesh to fathom in its fall.
Yet under tempest-lash and surfeitings
Some inmost sob, half-heard, dissuades the abyss,
Merges the wind in measure to the waves,

Series on series, infinite,—till eyes
Starved wide on blackened tides, accrete—enclose
This turning rondure whole, this crescent ring
Sun-cusped and zoned with modulated fire
Like pearls that whisper through the Doge's hands
—Yet no delirium of jewels! O Fernando,
Take of that eastern shore, this western sea,
Yet yield thy God's, thy Virgin's charity!

—Rush down the plenitude, and you shall see
Isaiah counting famine on this lee!

*

An herb, a stray branch among salty teeth,
The jellied weeds that drag the shore,—perhaps

Tomorrow's moon will grant us Saltes Bar—
Palos again,—a land cleared of long war.
Some Angelus environs the cordage tree;
Dark waters onward shake the dark prow free.

*

O Thou who sleepest on Thyself, apart
Like ocean athwart lanes of death and birth,
And all the eddying breath between dost search
Cruelly with love thy parable of man,—
Inquisitor! incognizable Word
Of Eden and the enchained Sepulchre,
Into thy steep savannahs, burning blue,
Utter to loneliness the sail is true.

Who grindest oar, and arguing the mast
Subscribest holocaust of ships, O Thou
Within whose primal scan consummately
The glistening seignories of Ganges swim;—
Who sendest greeting by the corposant,
And Teneriffe's garnet—flamed it in a cloud,
Urging through night our passage to the Chan;—
Te Deum laudamus, for thy teeming span!

Of all that amplitude that time explores,
A needle in the sight, suspended north,—
Yielding by inference and discard, faith
And true appointment from the hidden shoal:
This disposition that thy night relates
From Moon to Saturn in one sapphire wheel:
The orbic wake of thy once whirling feet,
Elohim, still I hear thy sounding heel!

White toil of heaven's cordons, mustering
In holy rings all sails charged to the far
Hushed gleaming fields and pendant seething wheat
Of knowledge,—round thy brows unhooded now

—The kindled Crown! acceded of the poles
And biassed by full sails, meridians reel
Thy purpose—still one shore beyond desire!
The sea's green crying towers a-sway, Beyond

And kingdoms
          naked in the
                 trembling heart—
      Te Deum laudamus
                  O Thou Hand of Fire

The Tunnel

To Find the Western path
Right thro' the Gates of Wrath.

BLAKE

Performances, assortments, résumés—
Up Times Square to Columbus Circle lights
Channel the congresses, nightly sessions,
Refractions of the thousand theatres, faces—
Mysterious kitchens. . . . You shall search them all.
Someday by heart you'll learn each famous sight
And watch the curtain lift in hell's despite;
You'll find the garden in the third act dead,
Finger your knees—and wish yourself in bed
With tabloid crime-sheets perched in easy sight.

Then let you reach your hat
and go.
As usual, let you—also
walking down—exclaim
to twelve upward leaving
a subscription praise
for what time slays.

Or can't you quite make up your mind to ride;
A walk is better underneath the L a brisk
Ten blocks or so before? But you find yourself
Preparing penguin flexions of the arms,—
As usual you will meet the scuttle yawn:
The subway yawns the quickest promise home.

Be minimum, then, to swim the hiving swarms
Out of the Square, the Circle burning bright—
Avoid the glass doors gyring at your right,
Where boxed alone a second, eyes take fright
—Quite unprepared rush naked back to light:
And down beside the turnstile press the coin
Into the slot. The gongs already rattle.

And so
of cities you bespeak
subways, rivered under streets
and rivers. . . . In the car
the overtone of motion
underground, the monotone
of motion is the sound
of other faces, also underground—

"Let's have a pencil Jimmy—living now
at Floral Park
Flatbush—on the fourth of July—
like a pigeon's muddy dream—potatoes
to dig in the field—travlin the town—too—
night after night—the Culver line—the
girls all shaping up—it used to be—"

Our tongues recant like beaten weather vanes.
This answer lives like verdigris, like hair
Beyond extinction, surcease of the bone;
And repetition freezes—"What

"what do you want? getting weak on the links?
fandaddle daddy don't ask for change—IS THIS
FOURTEENTH? it's half past six she said—if
you don't like my gate why did you
swing on it, why *didja*
swing on it
anyhow—"

And somehow anyhow swing—

The phonographs of hades in the brain
Are tunnels that re-wind themselves, and love
A burnt match skating in a urinal—
Somewhere above Fourteenth TAKE THE EXPRESS
To brush some new presentiment of pain—

"But I want service in this office SERVICE
I said—after
the show she cried a little afterwards but—"

Whose head is swinging from the swollen strap?
Whose body smokes along the bitten rails,
Bursts from a smoldering bundle far behind
In back forks of the chasms of the brain,—
Puffs from a riven stump far out behind
In interborough fissures of the mind . . . ?

And why do I often meet your visage here,
Your eyes like agate lanterns—on and on
Below the toothpaste and the dandruff ads?
—And did their riding eyes right through your side,
And did their eyes like unwashed platters ride?
And Death, aloft,—gigantically down
Probing through you—toward me, O evermore!
And when they dragged your retching flesh,
Your trembling hands that night through Baltimore—
That last night on the ballot rounds, did you
Shaking, did you deny the ticket, Poe?

For Gravesend Manor change at Chambers Street.
The platform hurries along to a dead stop.

The intent escalator lifts a serenade
Stilly
Of shoes, umbrellas, each eye attending its shoe, then
Bolting outright somewhere above where streets

Burst suddenly in rain. . . . The gongs recur:
Elbows and levers, guard and hissing door.
Thunder is galvothermic here below. . . . The car
Wheels off. The train rounds, bending to a scream,
Taking the final level for the dive
Under the river—
And somewhat emptier than before,
Demented, for a hitching second, humps; then
Lets go. . . . Toward corners of the floor
Newspapers wing, revolve and wing.
Blank windows gargle signals through the roar.

And does the Dæmon take you home, also,
Wop washerwoman, with the bandaged hair?
After the corridors are swept, the cuspidors—
The gaunt sky-barracks cleanly now, and bare,
O Genoese, do you bring mother eyes and hands
Back home to children and to golden hair?

Dæmon, demurring and eventful yawn!
Whose hideous laughter is a bellows mirth
—Or the muffled slaughter of a day in birth—
O cruelly to inoculate the brinking dawn
With antennæ toward worlds that glow and sink;—
To spoon us out more liquid than the dim
Locution of the eldest star, and pack
The conscience navelled in the plunging wind,
Umbilical to call—and straightway die!

O caught like pennies beneath soot and steam,
Kiss of our agony thou gatherest;
Condensed, thou takest all—shrill ganglia
Impassioned with some song we fail to keep.
And yet, like Lazarus, to feel the slope,
The sod and billow breaking,—lifting ground,
—A sound of waters bending astride the sky
Unceasing with some Word that will not die . . . !

*

A tugboat, wheezing wreaths of steam,
Lunged past, with one galvanic blare stove up the River.
I counted the echoes assembling, one after one,
Searching, thumbing the midnight on the piers.
Lights, coasting, left the oily tympanum of waters;
The blackness somewhere gouged glass on a sky.
And this thy harbor, O my City, I have driven under,
Tossed from the coil of ticking towers. . . .
          Tomorrow,
And to be. . . . Here by the River that is East—
Here at the waters' edge the hands drop memory;
Shadowless in that abyss they unaccounting lie.
How far away the star has pooled the sea—
Or shall the hands be drawn away, to die?

Kiss of our agony Thou gatherest,
          O Hand of Fire
              gatherest—

ATLANTIS

Music is then the knowledge of that which
relates to love in harmony and system.

PLATO

Through the bound cable strands, the arching path
Upward, veering with light, the flight of strings,—
Taut miles of shuttling moonlight syncopate
The whispered rush, telepathy of wires.
Up the index of night, granite and steel—
Transparent meshes—fleckless the gleaming staves—
Sibylline voices flicker, waveringly stream
As though a god were issue of the strings. . . .

And through that cordage, threading with its call
One arc synoptic of all tides below—
Their labyrinthine mouths of history
Pouring reply as though all ships at sea
Complighted in one vibrant breath made cry,—
"Make thy love sure—to weave whose song we ply!"
—From black embankments, moveless soundings hailed,
So seven oceans answer from their dream.

And on, obliquely up bright carrier bars
New octaves trestle the twin monoliths
Beyond whose frosted capes the moon bequeaths
Two worlds of sleep (O arching strands of song!)—
Onward and up the crystal-flooded aisle
White tempest nets file upward, upward ring
With silver terraces the humming spars,
The loft of vision, palladium helm of stars.

Sheerly the eyes, like seagulls stung with rime—
Slit and propelled by glistening fins of light—
Pick biting way up towering looms that press
Sidelong with flight of blade on tendon blade
—Tomorrows into yesteryear—and link
What cipher-script of time no traveller reads
But who, through smoking pyres of love and death,
Searches the timeless laugh of mythic spears.

Like hails, farewells—up planet-sequined heights
Some trillion whispering hammers glimmer Tyre:
Serenely, sharply up the long anvil cry
Of inchling æons silence rivets Troy.
And you, aloft there—Jason! hesting Shout!
Still wrapping harness to the swarming air!
Silvery the rushing wake, surpassing call,
Beams yelling Æolus! splintered in the straits!

From gulfs unfolding, terrible of drums,
Tall Vision-of-the-Voyage, tensely spare—
Bridge, lifting night to cycloramic crest
Of deepest day—O Choir, translating time
Into what multitudinous Verb the suns
And synergy of waters ever fuse, recast
In myriad syllables,—Psalm of Cathay!
O Love, thy white, pervasive Paradigm . . . !

We left the haven hanging in the night—
Sheened harbor lanterns backward fled the keel.
Pacific here at time's end, bearing corn,—
Eyes stammer through the pangs of dust and steel.
And still the circular, indubitable frieze
Of heaven's meditation, yoking wave
To kneeling wave, one song devoutly binds—
The vernal strophe chimes from deathless strings!

O Thou steeled Cognizance whose leap commits
The agile precincts of the lark's return;
Within whose lariat sweep encinctured sing
In single chrysalis the many twain,—

Of stars Thou art the stitch and stallion glow
And like an organ, Thou, with sound of doom—
Sight, sound and flesh Thou leadest from time's realm
As love strikes clear direction for the helm.

Swift peal of secular light, intrinsic Myth
Whose fell unshadow is death's utter wound,—
O River-throated—iridescently upborne
Through the bright drench and fabric of our veins;
With white escarpments swinging into light,
Sustained in tears the cities are endowed
And justified conclamant with ripe fields
Revolving through their harvests in sweet torment.

Forever Deity's glittering Pledge, O Thou
Whose canticle fresh chemistry assigns
To wrapt inception and beatitude,—
Always through blinding cables, to our joy,
Of thy white seizure springs the prophecy:
Always through spiring cordage, pyramids
Of silver sequel, Deity's young name
Kinetic of white choiring wings . . . ascends.

Migrations that must needs void memory,
Inventions that cobblestone the heart,—
Unspeakable Thou Bridge to Thee, O Love.
Thy pardon for this history, whitest Flower,
O Answerer of all,—Anemone,—
Now while thy petals spend the suns about us, hold—
(O Thou whose radiance doth inherit me)
Atlantis,—hold thy floating singer late!

So to thine Everpresence, beyond time,
Like spears ensanguined of one tolling star
That bleeds infinity—the orphic strings,
Sidereal phalanxes, leap and converge:
—One Song, one Bridge of Fire! Is it Cathay,
Now pity steeps the grass and rainbows ring
The serpent with the eagle in the leaves . . . ?
Whispers antiphonal in azure swing.

ALLEN GINSBERG

... lifting the city to Heaven which exists and is
everywhere about us!
Visions! omens! hallucinations! miracles!
ecstasies! gone down the American river!

"HOWL"

Allen Ginsberg

(United States, 1926–   )

Allen Ginsberg was born in Newark, New Jersey, and raised in Paterson, where the poet William Carlos Williams also lived. Ginsberg went to Columbia University, and it was there that he met Jack Kerouac, William Burroughs, and other writers who would come to be associated with the Beat era. In 1948, as Ginsberg was reflecting on what he should do with his life, he had an important revelation. A voice he recognized as William Blake's recited several Blake poems, and it seemed to the young poet that he had been allowed to peer into universal experience.

When Ginsberg's first book, *Howl*, was published in 1956, Williams's admiring introduction attempted to prepare the reader for the poems' extraordinary frankness, but this did not prevent the book's San Francisco publisher, Lawrence Ferlinghetti, from being tried for publishing an obscene book. Ferlinghetti was acquitted, and *Howl* went on to alter the landscape of American poetry. Critic Helen Vendler has said that Ginsberg was "responsible for loosening the breath of American poetry at mid century." Indeed, Ginsberg and other poets—John Ashbery, Gregory Corso, Robert Creeley, Robert Duncan, Lawrence Ferlinghetti, and Frank O'Hara, to name a handful—all fled the formal, academic verse of that period, breaking from "the tradition" in forms that spoke in a plain, more spontaneous and dynamic style.

Ginsberg's is a big voice that endeavors to speak to us all. Certainly "Howl," a record of the suffering of "the best minds of my generation" and a critique of postwar American society was, at the moment of its publication, one of the truly visionary poems of our century. Following in the well-trod steps of Whitman's "Song of the Open Road" and "Song of Myself," the poem is large in scope, radical in voice, generous in its caring and loving.

It is a poem with a vision that Ginsberg saw with ecstatic clarity. Williams wrote of it, "Poets are damned but they are not blind, they see through the eyes of the angels. This poet sees through and all around the horrors he partakes of in the very intimate details of his poem. He avoids nothing but experiences it to the hilt. He contains it. Claims it as his own."

Ginsberg has sought to engage the world around him in many ways, from his participation in leftist causes to his ongoing search for spiritual discipline and self-improvement by way of the principles of Buddhism. From the beginning he has professed a love of humanity in his life and work. He has traveled widely abroad as well as in the United States, where for many years his vigorous readings, intended to evoke a physical response in his audiences, as well as his generous interactions with them, have attracted very large crowds.

Ginsberg is surely the inheritor of Walt Whitman's flame, and he has, for the past forty years, carried it brightly. But in bringing around, and to a close, this selection of visionary poets, he also carries the wand of the earlier mystical poets—Rumi, Lalla, and Mirabai—who engaged their followers with their personal example as well as with their inspired presentation of a poetic vision.

AMERICA

America I've given you all and now I'm nothing.
America two dollars and twentyseven cents January 17, 1956.
I can't stand my own mind.
America when will we end the human war?
Go fuck yourself with your atom bomb.
I don't feel good don't bother me.
I won't write my poem till I'm in my right mind.
America when will you be angelic?
When will you take off your clothes?
When will you look at yourself through the grave?
When will you be worthy of your million Trotskyites?
America why are your libraries full of tears?
America when will you send your eggs to India?
I'm sick of your insane demands.
When can I go into the supermarket and buy what I need with
    my good looks?
America after all it is you and I who are perfect not the next
    world.
Your machinery is too much for me.
You made me want to be a saint.
There must be some other way to settle this argument.
Burroughs is in Tangiers I don't think he'll come back it's
    sinister.
Are you being sinister or is this some form of practical joke?
I'm trying to come to the point.
I refuse to give up my obsession.
America stop pushing I know what I'm doing.
America the plum blossoms are falling.
I haven't read the newspapers for months, everyday somebody
    goes on trial for murder.
America I feel sentimental about the Wobblies.

America I used to be a communist when I was a kid I'm not
		sorry.
I smoke marijuana every chance I get.
I sit in my house for days on end and stare at the roses in the
		closet.
When I go to Chinatown I get drunk and never get laid.
My mind is made up there's going to be trouble.
You should have seen me reading Marx.
My psychoanalyst thinks I'm perfectly right.
I won't say the Lord's Prayer.
I have mystical visions and cosmic vibrations.
America I still haven't told you what you did to Uncle Max
		after he came over from Russia.

I'm addressing you.
Are you going to let your emotional life be run by Time
		Magazine?
I'm obsessed by Time Magazine.
I read it every week.
Its cover stares at me every time I slink past the corner
		candystore.
I read it in the basement of the Berkeley Public Library.
It's always telling me about responsibility. Businessmen are
		serious. Movie producers are serious. Everybody's
		serious but me.
It occurs to me that I am America.
I am talking to myself again.

Asia is rising against me.
I haven't got a chinaman's chance.
I'd better consider my national resources.
My national resources consist of two joints of marijuana
		millions of genitals an unpublishable private literature
		that jetplanes 1400 miles an hour and
		twentyfive-thousand mental institutions.
I say nothing about my prisons nor the millions of
		underprivileged who live in my flowerpots under the
		light of five hundred suns.

I have abolished the whorehouses of France, Tangiers is the
    next to go.
My ambition is to be President despite the fact that I'm a
    Catholic.

America how can I write a holy litany in your silly mood?
I will continue like Henry Ford my strophes are as individual as
    his automobiles more so they're all different sexes.
America I will sell you strophes $2500 apiece $500 down on
    your old strophe
America free Tom Mooney
America save the Spanish Loyalists
America Sacco & Vanzetti must not die
America I am the Scottsboro boys.
America when I was seven momma took me to Communist Cell
    meetings they sold us garbanzos a handful per ticket a
    ticket costs a nickel and the speeches were free
    everybody was angelic and sentimental about the
    workers it was all so sincere you have no idea what a
    good thing the party was in 1835 Scott Nearing was a
    grand old man a real mensch Mother Bloor the
    Silk-strikers' Ewig-Weibliche made me cry I once saw the
    Yiddish orator Israel Amter plain. Everybody must have
    been a spy.
America you don't really want to go to war.
America it's them bad Russians.
Them Russians them Russians and them Chinamen. And them
    Russians.
The Russia wants to eat us alive. The Russia's power mad. She
    wants to take our cars from out our garages.
Her wants to grab Chicago. Her needs a Red *Reader's Digest*.
    Her wants our auto plants in Siberia. Him big
    bureaucracy running our fillingstations.
That no good. Ugh. Him make Indians learn read. Him need
    big black niggers. Hah. Her make us all work sixteen
    hours a day. Help.
America this is quite serious.

America this is the impression I get from looking in the
    television set.
America is this correct?
I'd better get right down to the job.
It's true I don't want to join the Army or turn lathes in precision
    parts factories, I'm nearsighted and psychopathic
    anyway.
America I'm putting my queer shoulder to the wheel.

A SUPERMARKET IN CALIFORNIA

What thoughts I have of you tonight, Walt Whitman, for I
  walked down the sidestreets under the trees with a
  headache self-conscious looking at the full moon.
In my hungry fatigue, and shopping for images, I went into
  the neon fruit supermarket, dreaming of your
  enumerations!
What peaches and what penumbras! Whole families
  shopping at night! Aisles full of husbands! Wives in the
  avocados, babies in the tomatoes!—and you, García
  Lorca, what were you doing down by the watermelons?

I saw you, Walt Whitman, childless, lonely old grubber,
  poking among the meats in the refrigerator and eyeing
  the grocery boys.
I heard you asking questions of each: Who killed the pork
  chops? What price bananas? Are you my Angel?
I wandered in and out of the brilliant stacks of cans
  following you, and followed in my imagination by the
  store detective.
We strode down the open corridors together in our solitary
  fancy tasting artichokes, possessing every frozen
  delicacy, and never passing the cashier.

Where are we going, Walt Whitman? The doors close in an
  hour. Which way does your beard point tonight?
(I touch your book and dream of our odyssey in the
  supermarket and feel absurd.)
Will we walk all night through solitary streets? The trees
  add shade to shade, lights out in the houses, we'll both
  be lonely.
Will we stroll dreaming of the lost America of love past
  blue automobiles in driveways, home to our silent
  cottage?

Ah, dear father, graybeard, lonely old courage-teacher,
    what America did you have when Charon quit poling his
    ferry and you got out on a smoking bank and stood
    watching the boat disappear on the black waters of
    Lethe?

SUNFLOWER SUTRA

I walked on the banks of the tincan banana dock and sat down
    under the huge shade of a Southern Pacific locomotive to
    look at the sunset over the box house hills and cry.
Jack Kerouac sat beside me on a busted rusty iron pole,
    companion, we thought the same thoughts of the soul,
    bleak and blue and sad-eyed, surrounded by the gnarled
    steel roots of trees of machinery.
The oily water on the river mirrored the red sky, sun sank on
    top of final Frisco peaks, no fish in that stream, no hermit
    in those mounts, just ourselves rheumy-eyed and
    hung-over like old bums on the riverbank, tired and
    wily.
Look at the Sunflower, he said, there was a dead gray shadow
    against the sky, big as a man, sitting dry on top of a pile
    of ancient sawdust—
—I rushed up enchanted—it was my first sunflower, memories
    of Blake—my visions—Harlem
and Hells of the Eastern rivers, bridges clanking Joes Greasy
    Sandwiches, dead baby carriages, black treadless tires
    forgotten and unretreaded, the poem of the riverbank,
    condoms & pots, steel knives, nothing stainless, only the
    dank muck and the razor-sharp artifacts passing into the
    past—
and the gray Sunflower poised against the sunset, crackly bleak
    and dusty with the smut and smog and smoke of olden
    locomotives in its eye—
corolla of bleary spikes pushed down and broken like a
    battered crown, seeds fallen out of its face,
    soon-to-be-toothless mouth of sunny air, sunrays
    obliterated on its hairy head like a dried wire spiderweb,
leaves stuck out like arms out of the stem, gestures from the

sawdust root, broke pieces of plaster fallen out of the
    black twigs, a dead fly in its ear,
Unholy battered old thing you were, my sunflower O my soul, I
    loved you then!
The grime was no man's grime but death and human
    locomotives,
all that dress of dust, that veil of darkened railroad skin, that
    smog of cheek, that eyelid of black mis'ry, that sooty
    hand or phallus or protuberance of artificial
    worse-than-dirt—industrial—modern—all that
    civilization spotting your crazy golden crown—
and those blear thoughts of death and dusty loveless eyes and
    ends and withered roots below, in the home-pile of sand
    and sawdust, rubber dollar bills, skin of machinery, the
    guts and innards of the weeping coughing car, the empty
    lonely tincans with their rusty tongues alack, what more
    could I name, the smoked ashes of some cock cigar, the
    cunts of wheelbarrows and the milky breasts of cars,
    wornout asses out of chairs & sphincters of
    dynamos—all these
entangled in your mummied roots—and you there standing
    before me in the sunset, all your glory in your form!
A perfect beauty of a sunflower! a perfect excellent lovely
    sunflower existence! a sweet natural eye to the new hip
    moon, woke up alive and excited grasping in the sunset
    shadow sunrise golden monthly breeze!
How many flies buzzed round you innocent of your grime,
    while you cursed the heavens of the railroad and your
    flower soul?
Poor dead flower? when did you forget you were a flower?
    when did you look at your skin and decide you were an
    impotent dirty old locomotive? the ghost of a
    locomotive? the specter and shade of a once powerful
    mad American locomotive?
You were never no locomotive, Sunflower, you were a
    sunflower!
And you Locomotive, you are a locomotive, forget me not!

So I grabbed up the skeleton thick sunflower and stuck it at my
     side like a scepter,
and deliver my sermon to my soul, and Jack's soul too, and
     anyone who'll listen,
—We're not our skin of grime, we're not our dread bleak dusty
     imageless locomotive, we're all golden sunflowers
     inside, blessed by our own seed & hairy naked
     accomplishment-bodies growing into mad black formal
     sunflowers in the sunset, spied on by our eyes under the
     shadow of the mad locomotive riverbank sunset Frisco
     hilly tincan evening sitdown vision.

The Change: *Kyoto–Tokyo Express*

Black Magicians
Come home: the pink meat image
    black yellow image with
    ten fingers and two eyes
is gigantic already: the black
    curly pubic hair, the
    blind hollow stomach,
the silent soft open vagina
    rare womb of new birth
cock lone and happy to be home
                   again
touched by hands by mouths,
    by hairy lips—

Close the portals of the festival?

Open the portals to what Is,
The mattress covered with sheets,
    soft pillows of skin,
long soft hair and delicate
    palms along the buttocks
    timidly touching,
waiting for a sign, a throb
    softness of balls, rough
    nipples alone in the dark
    met by a weird finger;

Tears allright, and laughter
    allright
I am that I am—

  Closed off from this
The schemes begin, roulette,
    brainwaves, bony dice,
    Stroboscope motorcycles
    Stereoscopic Scaly
       Serpents winding thru
          cloud spaces of
             what is not—

". . . convoluted, lunging upon
a pismire, a conflagration, a—"

II

Shit! Intestines boiling in sand fire
    creep yellow brain cold sweat
    earth unbalanced vomit thru
    tears, snot ganglia buzzing
    the Electric Snake rising hypnotic
    shuffling metal-eyed coils
    whirling rings within wheels
    from asshole up the spine
    Acid in the throat the chest
    a knot trembling Swallow back
    the black furry ball of the great
    Fear

Oh!

The serpent in my bed pitiful
    crawling unwanted babes of
    snake covered with veins and pores
    breathing heavy frightened love

metallic Bethlehem out the window
the lost, the lost hungry
ghosts here alive trapped
in carpet rooms   How can I
be sent to Hell
with my skin and blood

Oh I remember myself so

Gasping, staring at dawn over
lower Manhattan   the bridges
covered with rust, the slime
in my mouth & ass, sucking
his cock like a baby crying Fuck
me in my asshole   Make love
to this rotten slave   Give me the
power to whip & eat your heart
I own your belly & your eyes
I speak thru your screaming
mouth Black Mantra Fuck you
Fuck me Mother Brother Friend
old white haired creep shuddering in
the toilet slum bath floorboards—

Oh how wounded, how wounded, I
murder the beautiful chinese women

It will come on the railroad, beneath
the wheels, in drunken hate screaming
thru the skinny machine gun, it will
come out of the mouth of the pilot
the dry lipped diplomat, the hairy
teacher will come out of me
again shitting the meat out of
my ears on my cancer deathbed

Oh crying man crying woman
crying guerrilla shopkeeper

crying dysentery boneface on
the urinal street of the Self

Oh Negro beaten in the eye in my
home, oh black magicians
in white skin robes boiling the
stomachs of your children that
you do not die but shudder in
Serpent & worm shape forever
Powerful minds & superhuman
Roar of volcano & rocket in
Your bowels—

Hail to your fierce desire, your
Godly pride, my Heaven's gate
will not be closed until
we enter all—

All human shapes, all
trembling donkeys & apes, all
lovers turned to ghost
all achers on trains &
taxicab bodies sped away
from date with desire, old movies,
all who were refused—

All which was rejected, the
leper-sexed hungry of
nazi conventions, hollow
cheeked arab marxists of Acco
Crusaders dying of starvation
in the Holy Land—

Seeking the Great Spirit of the
Universe in Terrible Godly
form, O suffering Jews
burned in the hopeless fire
O thin Bengali sadhus adoring

Kali mother hung with
nightmare skulls O Myself
under her pounding
feet!

Yes I am that worm soul under
the heel of the daemon horses
I am that man trembling to die
in vomit & trance in bamboo
eternities belly ripped by
red hands of courteous
chinamen kids—Come sweetly
now back to my Self as I was—

Allen Ginsberg says this: I am
a mass of sores and worms
& baldness & belly & smell
I am false Name the prey
of Yamantaka Devourer of
Strange dreams, the prey of
radiation & Police Hells of Law

I am that I am I am the
man & the Adam of hair in
my loins   This is my spirit and
physical shape I inhabit
this Universe Oh weeping
against what is my
own nature for now

Who would deny his own shape's
loveliness in his
dream moment of bed
Who sees his desire to be
horrible instead of Him

Who is, who cringes, perishes,
is reborn a red Screaming

baby? Who cringes before
    that meaty shape in
        Fear?

In this dream I am the Dreamer
    and the Dreamed   I am
    that I am Ah but I have
    always known

oooh for the hate I have spent
    in denying my image & cursing
    the breasts of illusion—
    Screaming at murderers, trembling
    between their legs in fear of the
    steel pistols of my mortality—

Come, sweet lonely Spirit, back
    to your bodies, come great God
    back to your only image, come
    to your many eyes & breasts,
    come thru thought and
    motion up all your
    arms the great gesture of
    Peace & acceptance Abhaya
    Mudra Mudra of fearlessness
    Mudra of Elephant Calmed &
    war-fear ended forever!

The war, the war on Man, the
    war on woman, the ghost
    assembled armies vanish in
    their realms

Chinese American Bardo Thodols
    all the seventy hundred hells from
    Orleans to Algeria tremble
    with tender soldiers weeping

In Russia the young poets rise
     to kiss the soul of the revolution
     in Vietnam the body is burned
     to show the truth of only the
     body in Kremlin & White House
     the schemers draw back
     weeping from their schemes—

In my train seat I renounce
     my power, so that I do
     live I will die

Over for now the Vomit, cut
     up & pincers in the skull,
     fear of bones, grasp
     against man woman & babe.

Let the dragon of Death
     come forth from his
     picture in the whirling
     white clouds' darkness

And suck dream brains &
     claim these lambs for his
     meat, and let him feed
     and be other than I

Till my turn comes and I
     enter that maw and change
     to a blind rock covered
     with misty ferns that
     I am not all now

but a universe of skin and breath
     & changing thought and
     burning hand & softened
     heart in the old bed of
     my skin   From this single

birth reborn that I am
to be so—

My own Identity now nameless
neither man nor dragon or
God

but the dreaming Me full
of physical rays' tender
red moons in my belly &
Stars in my eyes circling

And the Sun the Sun the
Sun my visible father
making my body visible
thru my eyes!

WALES VISITATION

White fog lifting & falling on mountain-brow
    Trees moving in rivers of wind
                        The clouds arise
    as on a wave, gigantic eddy lifting mist
        above teeming ferns exquisitely swayed
                            along a green crag
        glimpsed thru mullioned glass in valley raine—

Bardic, O Self, Visitacione, tell naught
    but what seen by one man in a vale in Albion,
        of the folk, whose physical sciences end in Ecology,
            the wisdom of earthly relations,
        of mouths & eyes interknit ten centuries visible
            orchards of mind language manifest human,
    of the satanic thistle that raises its horned symmetry
        flowering above sister grass-daisies' pink tiny
            bloomlets angelic as lightbulbs—

Remember 160 miles from London's symmetrical thorned tower
        & network of TV pictures flashing bearded your Self
    the lambs on the tree-nooked hillside this day bleating
    heard in Blake's old ear, & the silent thought of Wordsworth
        in eld Stillness
    clouds passing through skeleton arches of Tintern Abbey—
        Bard Nameless as the Vast, babble to Vastness!

All the Valley quivered, one extended motion, wind
                undulating on mossy hills
    a giant wash that sank white fog delicately down red runnels
                on the mountainside
    whose leaf-branch tendrils moved asway
        in granitic undertow down—
and lifted the floating Nebulous upward, and lifted the arms of
        the trees

and lifted the grasses an instant in balance
        and lifted the lambs to hold still
    and lifted the green of the hill, in one solemn wave

A solid mass of Heaven, mist-infused, ebbs thru the vale,
    a wavelet of Immensity, lapping gigantic through Llanthony
        Valley,
the length of all England, valley upon valley under Heaven's
    ocean
                    tonned with cloud-hang,
            —Heaven balanced on a grassblade.
Roar of the mountain wind slow, sigh of the body,
        One Being on the mountainside stirring gently
            Exquisite scales trembling everywhere in balance,
    one motion thru the cloudy sky-floor shifting on the million
        feet of daisies,
one Majesty the motion that stirred wet grass quivering
        to the farthest tendril of white fog poured down
            through shivering flowers on the mountain's head—

No imperfection in the budded mountain,
        Valleys breathe, heaven and earth move together,
    daisies push inches of yellow air, vegetables tremble,
                grass shimmers green
sheep speckle the mountainside, revolving their jaws with
        empty eyes,
            horses dance in the warm rain,
        tree-lined canals network live farmland,
            blueberries fringe stone walls on hawthorn'd hills,
        pheasants croak on meadows haired with fern—
Out, out on the hillside, into the ocean sound, into delicate
        gusts of wet air,
Fall on the ground, O great Wetness, O Mother, No harm on
        your body!
Stare close, no imperfection in the grass,
        each flower Buddha-eye, repeating the story,
                myriad-formed—
Kneel before the foxglove raising green buds, mauve bells
        drooped

doubled down the stem trembling antennae,
& look in the eyes of the branded lambs that stare
breathing stockstill under dripping hawthorn—
I lay down mixing my beard with the wet hair of the
    mountainside,
    smelling the brown vagina-moist ground, harmless,
        tasting the violet thistle-hair, sweetness—
One being so balanced, so vast, that its softest breath
    moves every floweret in the stillness on the valley floor,
   trembles lamb-hair hung gossamer rain-beaded in the grass,
Lifts trees on their roots, birds in the great draught
    hiding their strength in the rain, bearing same weight,

Groan thru breast and neck, a great Oh! to earth heart
    Calling our Presence together
    The great secret is no secret
    Senses fit the winds,
      Visible is visible,
    rain-mist curtains wave through the bearded vale,
     gray atoms wet the wind's kabbala
Crosslegged on a rock in dusk rain,
    rubber booted in soft grass, mind moveless,
   breath trembles in white daisies by the roadside,
    Heaven breath and my own symmetric
    Airs wavering thru antlered green fern
drawn in my navel, same breath as breathes thru Capel-Y-Ffn,
    Sounds of Aleph and Aum
     through forests of gristle,
    my skull and Lord Hereford's Knob equal,
    All Albion one.

What did I notice? Particulars! The
    vision of the great One is myriad—
smoke curls upward from ashtray,
    house fire burned low,
The night, still wet & moody black heaven
    starless
    upward in motion with wet wind.

HOWL

(For Carl Solomon)

I

I saw the best minds of my generation destroyed by madness,
        starving hysterical naked,
dragging themselves through the negro streets at dawn looking
        for an angry fix,
angelheaded hipsters burning for the ancient heavenly
        connection to the starry dynamo in the machinery of
        night,
who poverty and tatters and hollow-eyed and high sat up
        smoking in the supernatural darkness of cold-water flats
        floating across the tops of cities contemplating jazz,
who bared their brains to Heaven under the El and saw
        Mohammedan angels staggering on tenement roofs
        illuminated,
who passed through universities with radiant cool eyes
        hallucinating Arkansas and Blake-light tragedy among
        the scholars of war,
who were expelled from the academies for crazy & publishing
        obscene odes on the windows of the skull,
who cowered in unshaven rooms in underwear, burning their
        money in wastebaskets and listening to the Terror
        through the wall,
who got busted in their pubic beards returning through Laredo
        with a belt of marijuana for New York,
who ate fire in paint hotels or drank turpentine in Paradise
        Alley, death, or purgatoried their torsos night after night
with dreams, with drugs, with waking nightmares, alcohol and
        cock and endless balls,
incomparable blind streets of shuddering cloud and lightning

in the mind leaping toward poles of Canada & Paterson,
     illuminating all the motionless world of Time between,
Peyote solidities of halls, backyard green tree cemetery dawns,
     wine drunkenness over the rooftops, storefront boroughs
     of teahead joyride neon blinking traffic light, sun and
     moon and tree vibrations in the roaring winter dusks of
     Brooklyn, ashcan rantings and kind king light of mind,
who chained themselves to subways for the endless ride from
     Battery to holy Bronx on benzedrine until the noise of
     wheels and children brought them down shuddering
     mouth-wracked and battered bleak of brain all drained
     of brilliance in the drear light of Zoo,
who sank all night in submarine light of Bickford's floated out
     and sat through the stale beer afternoon in desolate
     Fugazzi's, listening to the crack of doom on the
     hydrogen jukebox,
who talked continuously seventy hours from park to pad to bar
     to Bellevue to museum to the Brooklyn Bridge,
a lost battalion of platonic conversationalists jumping down the
     stoops off fire escapes off windowsills off Empire State
     out of the moon,
yacketayakking screaming vomiting whispering facts and
     memories and anecdotes and eyeball kicks and shocks of
     hospitals and jails and wars,
whole intellects disgorged in total recall for seven days and
     nights with brilliant eyes, meat for the Synagogue cast on
     the pavement,
who vanished into nowhere Zen New Jersey leaving a trail of
     ambiguous picture postcards of Atlantic City Hall,
suffering Eastern sweats and Tangerian bone-grindings and
     migraines of China under junk-withdrawal in Newark's
     bleak furnished room,
who wandered around and around at midnight in the railroad
     yard wondering where to go, and went, leaving no
     broken hearts,
who lit cigarettes in boxcars boxcars boxcars racketing through
     snow toward lonesome farms in grandfather night,
who studied Plotinus Poe St. John of the Cross telepathy and

bop kabbalah because the cosmos instinctively vibrated
at their feet in Kansas,
who loned it through the streets of Idaho seeking visionary
indian angels who were visionary indian angels,
who thought they were only mad when Baltimore gleamed in
supernatural ecstasy,
who jumped in limousines with the Chinaman of Oklahoma on
the impulse of winter midnight streetlight smalltown
rain,
who lounged hungry and lonesome through Houston seeking
jazz or sex or soup, and followed the brilliant Spaniard
to converse about America and Eternity, a hopeless task,
and so took ship to Africa,
who disappeared into the volcanoes of Mexico leaving behind
nothing but the shadow of dungarees and the lava and
ash of poetry scattered in fireplace Chicago,
who reappeared on the West Coast investigating the FBI in
beards and shorts with big pacifist eyes sexy in their
dark skin passing out incomprehensible leaflets,
who burned cigarette holes in their arms protesting the narcotic
tobacco haze of Capitalism,
who distributed Supercommunist pamphlets in Union Square
weeping and undressing while the sirens of Los Alamos
wailed them down, and wailed down Wall, and the
Staten Island ferry also wailed,
who broke down crying in white gymnasiums naked and
trembling before the machinery of other skeletons,
who bit detectives in the neck and shrieked with delight in
policecars for committing no crime but their own wild
cooking pederasty and intoxication,
who howled on their knees in the subway and were dragged off
the roof waving genitals and manuscripts,
who let themselves be fucked in the ass by saintly
motorcyclists, and screamed with joy,
who blew and were blown by those human seraphim, the
sailors, caresses of Atlantic and Caribbean love,
who balled in the morning in the evenings in rosegardens and
the grass of public parks and cemeteries scattering their
semen freely to whomever come who may,

who hiccuped endlessly trying to giggle but wound up with a
     sob behind a partition in a Turkish Bath when the blond
     & naked angel came to pierce them with a sword,
who lost their loveboys to the three old shrews of fate the one
     eyed shrew of the heterosexual dollar the one eyed
     shrew that winks out of the womb and the one eyed
     shrew that does nothing but sit on her ass and snip the
     intellectual golden threads of the craftsman's loom,
who copulated ecstatic and insatiate with a bottle of beer a
     sweetheart a package of cigarettes a candle and fell off
     the bed, and continued along the floor and down the hall
     and ended fainting on the wall with a vision of ultimate
     cunt and come eluding the last gyzym of consciousness,
who sweetened the snatches of a million girls trembling in the
     sunset, and were red eyed in the morning but prepared
     to sweeten the snatch of the sunrise, flashing buttocks
     under barns and naked in the lake,
who went out whoring through Colorado in myriad stolen
     night-cars, N.C., secret hero of these poems, cocksman
     and Adonis of Denver—joy to the memory of his
     innumerable lays of girls in empty lots & diner
     backyards, moviehouses' rickety rows, on mountaintops
     in caves or with gaunt waitresses in familiar roadside
     lonely petticoat upliftings & especially secret gas-station
     solipsisms of johns, & hometown alleys too,
who faded out in vast sordid movies, were shifted in dreams,
     woke on a sudden Manhattan, and picked themselves up
     out of basements hung-over with heartless Tokay and
     horrors of Third Avenue iron dreams & stumbled to
     unemployment offices,
who walked all night with their shoes full of blood on the
     snowbank docks waiting for a door in the East River to
     open to a room full of steamheat and opium,
who created great suicidal dramas on the apartment cliff-banks
     of the Hudson under the wartime blue floodlight of the
     moon & their heads shall be crowned with laurel in
     oblivion,
who ate the lamb stew of the imagination or digested the crab
     at the muddy bottom of the rivers of Bowery,

who wept at the romance of the streets with their pushcarts full
　　　　of onions and bad music,
who sat in boxes breathing in the darkness under the bridge,
　　　　and rose up to build harpsichords in their lofts,
who coughed on the sixth floor of Harlem crowned with flame
　　　　under the tubercular sky surrounded by orange crates of
　　　　theology,
who scribbled all night rocking and rolling over lofty
　　　　incantations which in the yellow morning were stanzas
　　　　of gibberish,
who cooked rotten animals lung heart feet tail borsht & tortillas
　　　　dreaming of the pure vegetable kingdom,
who plunged themselves under meat trucks looking for an egg,
who threw their watches off the roof to cast their ballot for
　　　　Eternity outside of Time, & alarm clocks fell on their
　　　　heads every day for the next decade,
who cut their wrists three times successively unsuccessfully,
　　　　gave up and were forced to open antique stores where
　　　　they thought they were growing old and cried,
who were burned alive in their innocent flannel suits on
　　　　Madison Avenue amid blasts of leaden verse & the
　　　　tanked-up clatter of the iron regiments of fashion & the
　　　　nitroglycerine shrieks of the fairies of advertising & the
　　　　mustard gas of sinister intelligent editors, or were run
　　　　down by the drunken taxicabs of Absolute Reality,
who jumped off the Brooklyn Bridge this actually happened
　　　　and walked away unknown and forgotten into the
　　　　ghostly daze of Chinatown soup alleyways & firetrucks,
　　　　not even one free beer,
who sang out of their windows in despair, fell out of the
　　　　subway window, jumped in the filthy Passaic, leaped on
　　　　negroes, cried all over the street, danced on broken
　　　　wineglasses barefoot smashed phonograph records of
　　　　nostalgic European 1930s German jazz finished the
　　　　whiskey and threw up groaning into the bloody toilet,
　　　　moans in their ears and the blast of colossal
　　　　steamwhistles,

who barreled down the highways of the past journeying to each
       other's hotrod-Golgotha jail-solitude watch or
       Birmingham jazz incarnation,
who drove crosscountry seventytwo hours to find out if I had a
       vision or you had a vision or he had a vision to find out
       Eternity,
who journeyed to Denver, who died in Denver, who came back
       to Denver & waited in vain, who watched over Denver &
       brooded & loned in Denver and finally went away to
       find out the Time, & now Denver is lonesome for her
       heroes,
who fell on their knees in hopeless cathedrals praying for each
       other's salvation and light and breasts, until the soul
       illuminated its hair for a second,
who crashed through their minds in jail waiting for impossible
       criminals with golden heads and the charm of reality in
       their hearts who sang sweet blues to Alcatraz,
who retired to Mexico to cultivate a habit, or Rocky Mount to
       tender Buddha or Tangiers to boys or Southern Pacific to
       the black locomotive or Harvard to Narcissus to
       Woodlawn to the daisychain or grave,
who demanded sanity trials accusing the radio of hypnotism &
       were left with their insanity & their hands & a hung jury,
who threw potato salad at CCNY lecturers on Dadaism and
       subsequently presented themselves on the granite steps
       of the madhouse with shaven heads and harlequin
       speech of suicide, demanding instantaneous lobotomy,
and who were given instead the concrete void of insulin
       Metrazol electricity hydrotherapy psychotherapy
       occupational therapy pingpong & amnesia,
who in humorless protest overturned only one symbolic
       pingpong table, resting briefly in catatonia,
returning years later truly bald except for a wig of blood, and
       tears and fingers, to the visible madman doom of the
       wards of the madtowns of the East,
Pilgrim State's Rockland's and Greystone's foetid halls,
       bickering with the echoes of the soul, rocking and rolling
       in the midnight solitude-bench dolmen-realms of love,

dream of life a nightmare, bodies turned to stone as
      heavy as the moon,
with mother finally ******, and the last fantastic book flung out
      of the tenement window, and the last door closed at 4
      A.M. and the last telephone slammed at the wall in reply
      and the last furnished room emptied down to the last
      piece of mental furniture, a yellow paper rose twisted on
      a wire hanger in the closet, and even that imaginary,
      nothing but a hopeful little bit of hallucination—
ah, Carl, while you are not safe I am not safe, and now you're
      really in the total animal soup of time—
and who therefore ran through the icy streets obsessed with a
      sudden flash of the alchemy of the use of the ellipse the
      catalog the meter & the vibrating plane,
who dreamt and made incarnate gaps in Time & Space through
      images juxtaposed, and trapped the archangel of the soul
      between 2 visual images and joined the elemental verbs
      and set the noun and dash of consciousness together
      jumping with sensation of Pater Omnipotens Aeterna
      Deus
to recreate the syntax and measure of poor human prose and
      stand before you speechless and intelligent and shaking
      with shame, rejected yet confessing out the soul to
      conform to the rhythm of thought in his naked and
      endless head,
the madman bum and angel beat in Time, unknown, yet
      putting down here what might be left to say in time
      come after death,
and rose reincarnate in the ghostly clothes of jazz in the
      goldhorn shadow of the band and blew the suffering of
      America's naked mind for love into an eli eli lamma
      lamma sabacthani saxophone cry that shivered the cities
      down to the last radio
with the absolute heart of the poem of life butchered out of
      their own bodies good to eat a thousand years.

II

What sphinx of cement and aluminum bashed open their skulls
    and ate up their brains and imagination?
Moloch! Solitude! Filth! Ugliness! Ashcans and unobtainable
    dollars! Children screaming under the stairways! Boys
    sobbing in armies! Old men weeping in the parks!
Moloch! Moloch! Nightmare of Moloch! Moloch the loveless!
    Mental Moloch! Moloch the heavy judger of men!
Moloch the incomprehensible prison! Moloch the crossbone
    soulless jailhouse and Congress of sorrows! Moloch
    whose buildings are judgment! Moloch the vast stone of
    war! Moloch the stunned governments!
Moloch whose mind is pure machinery! Moloch whose blood is
    running money! Moloch whose fingers are ten armies!
    Moloch whose breast is a cannibal dynamo! Moloch
    whose ear is a smoking tomb!
Moloch whose eyes are a thousand blind windows! Moloch
    whose skyscrapers stand in the long streets like endless
    Jehovahs! Moloch whose factories dream and croak in
    the fog! Moloch whose smokestacks and antennae crown
    the cities!
Moloch whose love is endless oil and stone! Moloch whose soul
    is electricity and banks! Moloch whose poverty is the
    specter of genius! Moloch whose fate is a cloud of sexless
    hydrogen! Moloch whose name is the Mind!
Moloch in whom I sit lonely! Moloch in whom I dream Angels!
    Crazy in Moloch! Cocksucker in Moloch! Lacklove and
    manless in Moloch!
Moloch who entered my soul early! Moloch in whom I am a
    consciousness without a body! Moloch who frightened
    me out of my natural ecstasy! Moloch whom I abandon!
    Wake up in Moloch! Light streaming out of the sky!
Moloch! Moloch! Robot apartments! invisible suburbs! skeleton

treasuries! blind capitals! demonic industries! spectral
nations! invincible madhouses! granite cocks! monstrous
bombs!

They broke their backs lifting Moloch to Heaven! Pavements,
trees, radios, tons! lifting the city to Heaven which exists
and is everywhere about us!

Visions! omens! hallucinations! miracles! ecstasies! gone down
the American river!

Dreams! adorations! illuminations! religions! the whole
boatload of sensitive bullshit!

Breakthroughs! over the river! flips and crucifixions! gone
down the flood! Highs! Epiphanies! Despairs! Ten years'
animal screams and suicides! Minds! New loves! Mad
generation! down on the rocks of Time!

Real holy laughter in the river! They saw it all! the wild eyes!
the holy yells! They bade farewell! They jumped off the
roof! to solitude! waving! carrying flowers! Down to the
river! into the street!

III

Carl Solomon! I'm with you in Rockland
where you're madder than I am
I'm with you in Rockland
where you must feel very strange
I'm with you in Rockland
where you imitate the shade of my mother
I'm with you in Rockland
where you've murdered your twelve secretaries
I'm with you in Rockland
where you laugh at this invisible humor
I'm with you in Rockland
where we are great writers on the same dreadful typewriter
I'm with you in Rockland
where your condition has become serious and is reported on
the radio

I'm with you in Rockland
where the faculties of the skull no longer admit the worms of
        the senses
I'm with you in Rockland
where you drink the tea of the breasts of the spinsters of Utica
I'm with you in Rockland
where you pun on the bodies of your nurses the harpies of the
        Bronx
I'm with you in Rockland
where you scream in a straightjacket that you're losing the
        game of the actual pingpong of the abyss
I'm with you in Rockland
where you bang on the catatonic piano the soul is innocent and
        immortal it should never die ungodly in an armed
        madhouse
I'm with you in Rockland
where fifty more shocks will never return your soul to its body
        again from its pilgrimage to a cross in the void
I'm with you in Rockland
where you accuse your doctors of insanity and plot the Hebrew
        socialist revolution against the fascist national Golgotha
I'm with you in Rockland
where you will split the heavens of Long Island and resurrect
        your living human Jesus from the superhuman tomb
I'm with you in Rockland
where there are twentyfive thousand mad comrades all
        together singing the final stanzas of the Internationale
I'm with you in Rockland
where we hug and kiss the United States under our bedsheets
        the United States that coughs all night and won't let us
        sleep
I'm with you in Rockland
where we wake up electrified out of the coma by our own
        souls' airplanes roaring over the roof they've come to
        drop angelic bombs the hospital illuminates
        itself   imaginary walls collapse   O skinny legions run

Allen Ginsberg   327

outside   O starry-spangled shock of mercy the eternal
        war is here   O victory forget your underwear we're free
I'm with you in Rockland
in my dreams you walk dripping from a sea-journey on the
        highway across America in tears to the door of my
        cottage in the Western night